Mayan Toltec Azte of Our Soul Life
A Full-Color Journey through Temples and Texts

John Van Auken
Author of Ancient Egyptian Visions
Director of the Edgar Cayce Foundation

Copyright © 2017 John Van Auken

Living in the Light
P.O. Box 4942
Virginia Beach VA 23454-0942 USA
JohnVanAuken.com
JohnVanAukenNewsletter@Gmail.com

Mesoamerican Proverb
"It is only by my hand, by my face, my heart, my spirit that either I will wither or I will bloom..."

Contents

Introduction:
- 4 – Mesoamerica
- 5 – Edgar Cayce

6 - The Maize God in Body and Spirit
- Our Roles in this Journey
- Higher Consciousness Training

9 - Chocolate - A Social Protocol

12 - Misunderstanding About Many Gods

14 - Misunderstanding about Cutting Hearts Out

20 - Often Unsung Greatness of the Mesoamericans

22 - Legends and Tales of Our Soul's Journey

33 - The Story of the Twins and Xquic (she-queek)

40 - Our Soul Story in the San Bartolo Mural

Teachings inside Temples & Pyramids:
- 49 – Monte Albán: Illusions of the Game of Life
- 56 – Palenqué: Out of Celestial Life into Physical Life
- 68 – Teotihuacán: Water & Fire, Baptism & Inspiration
- 72 – Uxmal: The Magician Within Us

81 - Seven Caves, Seven Races

82 - "Mom" Coatlicue - The "Shadow"

83 - Ancient Altars and Magnetism

90 - The Cycles of Time - Prophecy

96 - Life, Death, and Rebirth

99 - Upside-Downness

100 - Reincarnation

Introduction

Mesoamerica

You will see the term Mesoamerica, literally this word means "middle America" in Greek. Mesoamerica was a region and cultural area extending from central Mexico to Belize, including Guatemala, El Salvador, Honduras, Nicaragua, and northern Costa Rica. These lands were where the pre-Columbian societies flourished before the Spanish colonization of the Americas in the 15th and 16th centuries. Mesoamericans includes these peoples: Olmec, Zapotec, Mayan, Toltec, and Aztec. The wisdom teachings of these cultures began around 2000 BC to roughly 1200 AD, then faded away over the next 200 years. When the Spanish arrived, hardly any of the native peoples could read the classic texts of their ancestors. A few of the Spanish Friars attempted to gather and preserve the Mesoamerican texts and oral legends. The texts took a long time to decipher, and many people contributed to the ultimate breakthrough in understanding the glyphs and their meaning. In this book we'll approach the teachings from a metaphysical, spiritual perspective for soul growth and enlightenment. Of course we will not ignore earthly perspectives.

Key to Understanding these Concepts and Stories

Since many of the teachings and practices have to do with initiation into the secret teachings, it is helpful to approach this material as one seeking inner vision, intuition, and revelation. As an Initiate in the Temples you are encouraged to keep a JOURNAL of your thoughts, dreams, and feelings as you go through these concepts and allegorical stories – conveying hidden meanings using symbolic figures, actions, imagery, and events, which together aim to reveal a deeper moral, spiritual, or even political teaching related to our soul growth. Often these are directed toward our eternal life rather than this relatively brief incarnation.

As we progress through the temples and legends it is best to approach these trainings as we would dreams – *as Soul dreams!*

—*John Van Auken*

Introduction

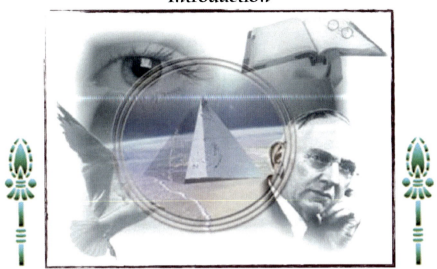

Edgar Cayce's Help

Edgar Cayce was the reincarnation of the ancient Egyptian High Priest Ra-Ta, and his readings of the Akashic Records convey concepts about us and our origin that are also found in many of the ancient teachings of the Mesoamericans. Here are some of Cayce's teachings:

Our true nature is, "as light, a ray that does not end, lives on and on, until it becomes one in essence with the source of light." (136-83)

"We find in the beginning, when the first of the elements were given, and the forces set in motion that brought about the sphere as we find called earth plane, and when the "Morning Stars" sang together (Job 38:7), and the whispering winds brought the news of the coming of man's indwelling, of the spirit of the Creator, becoming the living soul. This entity came into being with this multitude." (294-8)

"Not only God is God, but self is a part of that oneness." (900-181)

Our Purpose for Existing

Cayce helps us here too:

"The purpose is that you might know yourself to be yourself, and yet one with the Creative Forces, or God." (2030-1)

"Don't put the material first, for you have to live with yourself a long, long while! Become acquainted with yourself. Know yourself and the relationship to the Creative Forces." (3484-1) Of course the "self" he is referring to is our *immortal* soul. Immortality is eternal life, and that is a long, long while!

The Maize God in body and in spirit - 2 parts of Our Being

This image reveals how these two portions of our whole being may work together to bring us the seeds of enlightenment and well-being. Our eternal self and our temporal, physical self may work together. When they work together, they bring forth a better life and our more *ideal* self – our better self. As you can see in this image, they are feminine and masculine, anima and animus, yin and yang of our whole soul.

Work through these teachings at your own pace.

Remember the value of keeping a journal as you study and progress.

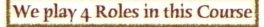

We play 4 Roles in this Course

In this virtual journey through the origins, influences, and destiny of life we play 4 roles:
1. a godling of the One God, i.e. a child of God,
2. a co-creator with God and the Creative Forces,
3. a ballplayer in the Game of Life,
4. and a Shaman-Priest or -Priestess.

Pottery Vessel ballgame - Chrysler Museum - Ballplayers in headdress and ritual costume.

The Maize god in spirit & body

Mayan - Toltec - Aztec
Higher Consciousness Training

Depictions on ancient walls, ceramics, and codices may be scenes of ritual ceremonies, historical events, mundane life, lineage records, even metaphors of oral traditions, and - important to us - images of myth and mysticism, which reveal the story of our soul's journey.

Mysticism contains the secrets of life beyond the physical but they affect the physical. Mysticism contains the secrets to higher states of consciousness and higher vibrations within our bodies and minds. Mysticism reveals other dimensions of life and influences affecting us from unseen sources.

Mayan scribes in codex-style depiction on vessel 69

Copyright 2014 © by John Van Auken

Higher Consciousness Training

This course seeks to explore and understand mysticism through the legends, rituals, and wisdom of Mesoamerica, particularly the mysticism of the
Maya, Toltecs, and Aztecs.

Unlike ancient Egyptian mysticism, the Mesoamericans deal more with the "Shadow Forces" of life. Therefore, the imagery depicted in this course contains some darkness and battles between good vs evil.

But there is also much beauty and civility to enjoy as well.

Codex showing the giving of a book as a gift.

Mesoamerican Proverb
Nya b'a'n tu'n t-xi tewin chib'aj cye tuliy,
ku'n ajo chib'aj b'e'x cy-elil× chuk-ix.
"It is not good to hide good food from visitors because it will turn into worms."

Civility and Social Custom
Cocoa - Chocolate - A Social Protocol

The Cacao (*ka-cow*) tree, called Madre Cacao and Theobroma Cacao, meaning "Food of the Gods" – a name coined by the Swedish botanist Carl Linnaeus from Greek "Theo" for god and "broma" for food – is native to the Americas, and was an important plant food in Mesoamerica.

The word *cacao* originated from the Olmec people and later from the Maya word *ka'kau'*, as well as the word *chocolate* from the Maya words *Chocol'ha* and the verb *chokola'j*, meaning "to drink chocolate together." Cacao was anglicized to *Cocoa* (some believe it was simply a misspelling of cacao!). These names were used later by the Aztecs. The Maya believed that the ka'kau' was discovered by the gods in a mountain that also contained other delectable foods used by the Maya. According to Mayan mythology, one of the Hero Twins gave cacao to the Maya after humans were created from maize (corn) by the divine grandmother goddess *Ixmucané* (pronounced, *eesh-MU-ca-nay*).

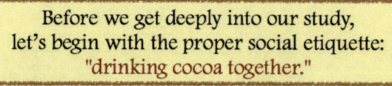
Before we get deeply into our study, let's begin with the proper social etiquette: "drinking cocoa together."

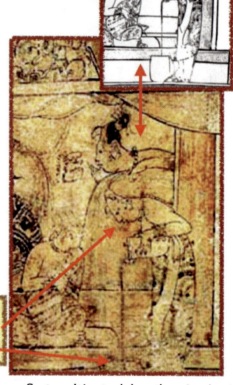

"maize cakes" (white corn bread)

Above: The host is checking the frothy, foam "Cacao" (English: cocoa).
Right: A woman is creating the frothy foam by pouring from a height that will create bubbles of air in the chocolate.

Chocolate was first cultivated by the Ancient Maya, however the way they consumed it was not like the sweet drink or treats we know today. Their preferred method of consumption was a thick, bitter, frothy drink, most often served cold. There are five or six basic ingredients that were likely used to make traditional Mayan Cacao: water, cacao, honey, vanilla, cinnamon, and chili pepper. The amount of each ingredient is uncertain. In some areas it is also traditional to combine this drink with corn meal, turning it into gruel to be consumed hot or cold. The true Mayan way to produce this drink was to pour the liquid from one vessel to another in order to create as much foam as possible. In some cases herbs were added to produce more foaming action.

When the Maize god dies and his soul ascends to heaven, his corpse is transformed into fruit trees and all the crops humans will eat. When the Maize god returns from death, he first rebirths himself as a Cacao tree.

Maize god's cycle

Statue of the Maize god.

Stylized Cacao Tree of the reincarnating Maize god

Remember, each human was originally created from maize, so the cycle of the Maize god reflects the cycle of each soul: birth, life, death, and then ultimately rebirth – first as chocolate (sweet baby) then as maize (adult human).

chokola'j: "Drinking Cocoa together."

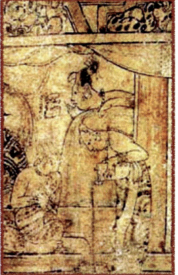

Now we can properly begin our study!

Misunderstanding About Many Gods

Despite the impression that all ancient theologies have many gods – gods for everything – if one digs deep enough there is always a singular, original god from which all god-like forces emerge. In the Mayan legends it is *Hunab Ku*, which literally means, "The Only One." Ultimately, in the midst of all the "manyness" and multiplicity, there is a Oneness – and that Oneness is in the infinite, original Creator.

The origin of Hunab Ku's symbol is unclear. It appears to have been an Aztec symbol rather than a Mayan one. There is some concern that Hunab Ku was a post-Spanish conquest concept, placating the conquerer's one-god theology. However, the *Popol Vuh* clearly has a singular creator referred to as "Heart of Heaven." All life came out of an original, singular oneness of creative expression. Here's the Aztec original:

The Only One

Notice a similarity to the Yin and Yang of ancient Taoism, dating back some 5,000 years ago. There is a dark side and a light side, and a little of light is in the dark side and a little of dark is in the light side.

The Aztec symbol is also similar to the The *inner circle* of the Nautilus

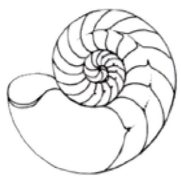

The Nautilus shell, lined with mother-of-pearl, grows into increasingly larger chambers throughout its life and so has become a symbol for expansion and renewal. Hunab Ku's symbol spirals out for its center, expanding to greater awareness, including the dark and light of the yin and yang.

Even in the mutli-gods of Egypt there is found an original, singular god named, *Atum*, meaning "The Complete One."

Misunderstanding About Cutting Hearts Out of People

We cannot immerse ourselves into the studies of the ancient Mayan, Toltec, and Aztec visions and wisdom (also Olmec, Zapotec, and Mixtec) without first addressing the disturbing practice of cutting hearts out of living people. Blood is in every aspect of ancient life, not just among the Mesoamericans. It is in most every ancient culture. The explanation is a bit complicated and rather difficult to understand given our perspective of life as we see it today, but here it goes:

Family gods, Bloodletting, and Death

These ancient peoples saw us as the Children of God. Out of an Infinite Oneness countless individuals were conceived, each given free will and each allowed to use their will to come to know themselves to be themselves while living within the Infinite Oneness, the Source of all Life. As the process of self-discovery or *individuation* continued, awareness of the Oneness became more difficult. The Collective Consciousness was fading as individual consciousness was growing and becoming more dominant. This resulted in a sense of aloneness and vulnerable to the forces of cause and effect, the karmic forces. As a result, the people turned increasingly to themselves and to those among them that appeared to be more powerful. Before long, the one god was replaced by many gods and goddesses. The Spirit and wisdom from the high heavens was gone. People sought help from the realms of their dead ancestors. It was believed that discarnate souls were nearer heaven than incarnates, so seeking their attention, guidance, and help was important. Altars to family or community gods were built. Early on, these discarnate souls did prove to be helpful, often speaking to their incarnate loved ones during ecstatic ceremonies designed to create altered states of consciousness among the incarnates. However, the more a person identified with matter and self-consciousness, the more they lost contact with the spirit world – and yet, they needed more *physical* help and protection. The descent into "manyness" and materialism continued until the forces of Nature became the primary power – making outer, physical life dangerous and difficult. One felt vulnerable. It became increasingly difficult for the discarnate ancestors to provide help because the incarnate individuals were becoming dull to spirit communication – they were too physical. Many attempts to regain the gods' and ancestors' attention were made by sacrificing foods, animals, and eventually *humans* on the altars.

It was believed that the soul of a *recently killed* person could enter the Netherworld while remaining semi-conscious to this world and give guidance to the people on Earth. Ceremonies were designed to take a pumping heart out of a sacrificial person, keeping them *semi-alive* in this world while becoming conscious in the other worlds. The priests began to teach that sacrificing a loved one, a virgin or a young person, would get the greater response from the gods or the discarnate family members – so reminiscent of biblical Abraham attempting to sacrifice his son Isaac to gain God's favor. Some victims actually offered themselves as a sacrifice, believing that they could help their families and tribal members. Conditions eventually got so dark that the sacrifice was only done to show physical power – most often using enemies as the victims.

Among ancient people, blood was believed to be *magical*, with a smell that not only attracted animals but also attracted the gods and spirits in the Netherworld. This belief in blood's magic caused the priests and priestesses to cut themselves, dripping their blood upon the altar to attract the gods or discarnate souls of their family and tribe. If anyone received help in this way, then the spot upon which it happened became sacred, and was honored by all and returned to many times in an effort to repeat the experience. Since blood had been a part of the ceremony, more blood would be shed trying to recreate the experience. In some cases, so much blood was shed that channels were built into the altars to carry the excess away.

The Mesoamericans were not the only people doing this. Blood sacrifice and bloodletting occurred among most ancient people. Even the Judeo-Christian religions have a legacy in blood sacrifice; from Abraham offering his son Isaac to the blood of Jesus Christ offered as an acceptable payment for humanity's sins.

Bloodletting rites were important religious and tribal events. The most sacred blood was said to come from the ear (*Tub*), tongue (*Ak'*), and penis (*Ach*). Piercing the ears was understood as opening to hear the divine oracle and experience a revelation. Cutting or piercing the tongue helped one speak what the gods said. Cutting the foreskin or penis was to join in divine procreation as co-creator with the gods. The blood was often spilled onto paper and then burned to affirm the cosmic balance of spirit first, flesh second. Maya used the Ek' Balam shrub (*Croton flavens L.*) to quickly seal the damaged blood vessels, or

the Bakalche' tree (*Bourreria pulchra Millsp.*) to close wounds in muscular tissue. Stingray spines were the most common instrument used to pierce and bleed.

In the image to the left a Mayan cuts his penis. In the image below a costumed priest pierces a person's tongue.

According to Edgar Cayce's reading of the Akashic records, members of the Lost Tribes of Israel actually landed in Yucatan, bringing their blood sacrifice ceremonies, these influence religious ceremonies in Yucatan. Some of these migrating "lost tribes" of Israel eventually ended up joining the Mound Builders in North America, specifically at Watson Brake and Poverty Point, Louisiana. According to archaeologists, Watson Brake was built around 3500 BC! Poverty Point was around 1650 BC. The Bat Creek Stone found in a mound in Tennessee has the words, "holy to Yahweh" inscribed on it in Paleo-Hebrew of the 1st century AD.

Refusing to accept blood sacrifice some Mesoamericans migrated northward to escape these aberrations of the original spiritual ceremonies. Some groups headed to Chaco Canyon and became cave dwellers. Others traveled up the Mississippi Valley and became the Mound Builders of North America.

Speaking mystically, death was viewed quite differently than we see it today. Souls, called the "Morning Stars" in the Bible (Job 38:7) were discarnate, immortal beings, so there was no death because the soul never died. Even this concept became distorted when some of these immortal minds so identified with their bodies that they felt that when their bodies died, they became wandering ghosts in the borderlands to the physical world. This was in spite of the widely accepted teaching of soul heavens.

According to Cayce's visions, souls initially entered this world in a Pacific Ocean region called *Lemuria*, whose name was *not* derived from the Lemur primates on Madagascar but from a Latin root word for "ghosts." The beginning of death as we know it today was a major downshift in consciousness. In order for an immortal soul to die, its mind had to so lose awareness of its connection with the eternal Source of Life that it actually believed that it did not exist beyond its *physical* body. When the mind completely identifies with matter, then the death of matter is the death of self. These souls had lost awareness of their eternal spirit-soul self.

Cayce taught that souls initially could maintain a degree of spirit awareness while living physically, and for many more years than we do today. This is why the ages of people in the early generations of the Bible legends were so very old. According to Cayce's reading of the Akashic record, there is no reason for a physical organism to age and die. With proper assimilation of nutrients needed by the body and eliminations of drosses and toxins that build up in a body, a physical organism should continue to regenerate, rejuvenate, and live; that is if the élan vital, the kundalini, the life force is actively *flowing* through the body. However, if the mind loses contact with the Life Force, then the body deteriorates, until it gives up the soul or ghost, and the mind and soul are forced to depart.

Once death became a part of life, then serious problems developed. Ceremonies were created to prepare for death, to take care of the corpse after death, and even to contact the deceased soul-mind in the realm beyond this one. Two excellent examples of ceremonies preparing one to die and enter the so-called "borderland" or Netherworld, and successfully traverse it are found in the Tibetan and Egyptian *Book of the Dead*. Both of these ancient texts outline the journey through various states of consciousness, realms of the Underworld, and hopefully on up to the Heavens. But increasing numbers of souls were not reaching the higher levels of life, living instead as ghosts in the borderlands to this material world.

On the next page is a stylized carving at El Tajin, in Veracruz, Mexico, depicting an individual in the sacred act of drawing blood from his penis. Notice that the figure in the water below receiving the blood wears a fish headdress, which may be a symbolic reference to the mind of the soul beneath the surface consciousness. Above the bleeder are images of dimensions beyond the third dimension and to the left slight we see a white being, perhaps symbolizing the godly self – 3 states: conscious, subconscious, and super conscious. Also notice the tiny mushrooms on the tree limb. Mushrooms were often used to help create the altered state of consciousness necessary to commune with the supernatural Life Forces and endure the pain of bloodletting. There were several potions used to assist in communing with supernatural dimensions, and in making a death-like initiation easier, as well as actual death easier. The drug culture of the 1960s may have been *reincarnating* souls from these previous cultures (see p. 100), and as such would have experienced the hallucinogenic states in their previous incarnations, and naturally seek to recreate those experiences in this life.

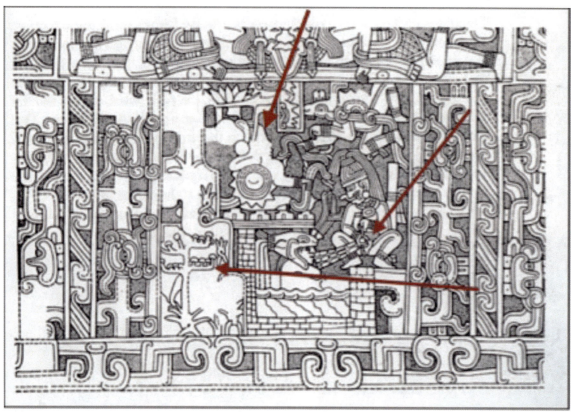

The top arrow points to white being, next arrow points to the bloodletting penis flowing to the fish-headed being in the water. The bottom arrow points to the mushrooms, used to reduce pain and create an altered state of consciousness.

The Legend that May Have Started the Cutting Out of Hearts

How did Mesoamericans get involved in the ritual of cutting hearts out of living bodies? They misunderstood an ancient tale. That tale begins with the legend of the Bird-Serpent god (*Quetzalcoatl* in Aztec, *Kukulkan* in Yucatec Mayan, and *Gucumatz* in Quiché Mayan) engaging the Children of God. In this story, the Bird-Serpent god, symbolizing the kundalini life force within the body (the serpent) and the higher mind (the bird that can fly high above it all) called all the Children of God together in preparation for the soul journey through Earth lifetimes – realizing that the souls had become possessed by physicality, selfishness, and lost to the Spirit. The Bird-Serpent god explained that the light had dimmed, leaving earth in darkness. He asked for a volunteer to be a fresh light to the Earth. Of course the most beautiful and egotistical of the Children came forward, because he was truly the perfect one for the job. The Bird-Serpent god then built a sacred fire, and instructed the beautiful one to jump into the fire to fulfill this mission. But he could not sacrifice his beauty, and backed away. Then the plain-looking, lowest one among the Children came forward and jumped into the fire. All the Children of God ran to the edge of heaven and looked down upon the Earth to see the Sun break through the darkness! What a brilliant light! Distraught at his missed opportunity, the beautiful one ran over and jumped into the fire. All the Children ran to the edge of heaven and looked down upon the Earth to see the Moon appear. Then they giggled because it is not as bright a light as the Sun. The moral being that humility and selflessness provide the brighter light, egotism only reflects the true light. Then, the Bird-Serpent god then told all of the Children that each of them must put *their hearts* into the sacred fire for this soul-saving effort to succeed. They put their hearts into the sacred fire. When finished, they ran to the edge of heaven to see all the stars appear! Each selfless heart was a star in the heavens.

Now you can easily see how unenlightened leaders could lose the original meaning of offering your heart to help humanity, and foolishly begin cutting hearts out as offerings.

Blood Sacrifice

Continuing confusion over blood sacrifice is seen when Jesus was discussing concepts of spirituality at the Temple of Solomon in Jerusalem, and a scribe working at the temple overheard the discussions and asked Jesus what commandment was most important. Now you must understand that blood sacrifices were going on at this temple. In fact, the first altar was called "place of slaughter" where an animal's blood would pour down the altar sides and the carcass was burned on top of the altar. Here's the quote:

"One of the scribes came up and heard them disputing with one another, and seeing that he (Jesus) answered them well, asked him, 'Which commandment is the first of all?' Jesus answered, 'The first is, Hear, O Israel; The Lord our God, the Lord is one; and you shall love the Lord your God with all your heart, and with all your soul, and with all your mind, and with all your strength. The second is this, You shall love your neighbor as yourself. There is no other commandment greater than these.' And the scribe said to him, 'You are right, Teacher; you have truly said that He is one, and there is no other but He; and to love Him with all the heart, and with all the understanding, and with all the strength, and to love one's neighbor as oneself, is much more than all whole burnt offerings and

The Sacrificial Altar of Solomon's Temple

sacrifices.' And when Jesus saw that he answered wisely, said to him, 'You are not far from the kingdom of God.' And after that no one dared to ask him (Jesus) any question." (Mark 6:28-34)

As you can see, Jesus perceives how spiritually enlightened the scribe is, and affirms his wisdom concerning burnt offerings and blood sacrifices as not being the ultimate way to spirituality, rather it is *love*. Despite this, blood sacrifice and bloodletting are found in Judeo-Christian lore. In Hebrews 9:22 we find, "Without shedding of blood there is no remission [of sin]." In the Epistle written by the apostle John we find: "The blood of Jesus Christ God's Son cleanses us from all sin." (I John 1:7) In Revelation 1:5 we read this: "To Him who loved us, and washed us from our sins in His own blood."

The story of Jesus and his ritual of Holy Communion – *"hic est sanguis meus"* meaning "this is my blood" – indicated that the drinking of Jesus' blood brought cleansing and renewal. However, in place of blood Jesus used wine, revealing a deeper truth. And that truth may have been the same that the Bird-Serpent god meant when instructing the Children of God to put their hearts into the sacred fire to rekindle light in the world of lost souls: Come together in a selfless cooperation to expand the consciousness and raise the vibrations of each and every soul so that the "Morning Stars" awaken again to who they truly are and what their ultimate destiny is. The Children's souls are the stars, the lights of heaven. Jesus also used a parable of branches on a grape vine to symbolized souls reconnecting to the vine of life in loving cooperation and thereby renewing their light.

Edgar Cayce conveyed that crucifixion was the crucifying of ones selfish desires in order that the greater, truer light and life may flow in and through oneself. He also gave a past-life for a woman who was a reincarnated Mayan priestess who innately knew that the growing movement toward cutting hearts out was wrong and a distortion of a deeper truth. Believing that the leaders had lost their connection to the Original Spirit, this priestess took her people out of the greater tribe and led her group up the Mississippi Valley to become some of the early Mound Builders. She and her people joined with people from other regions, who were also seeking a wiser life, a wiser way. Archaeologists estimate the there were once tens of thousands of human-made mounds in the U.S. – some dating back as far as 5,000 years ago!

Often Unsung Greatness of the Mesoamericans

Authentic Maya states: "The Maya were much more intellectually inclined than most archaeologists or anthropologists have indicated when they stress the wars between the cities or the rituals of blood sacrifice by the leaders, kings, and priesthood. The Mayan culture also was preoccupied with science, art, government, marketing, philosophy, letters and health. The Mayas were also involved in the scientific evaluation of medicinal applications to curing what ailed them, some 1500 different plants were used for herbal prescriptions. A civilization so robust and filled with great structure and fine aesthetic touch cannot reach such high levels of advancement unless it is well fed physically *and spiritually*." –authenticmaya.com

Medicine among the Maya was a blend of spirituality and science. The Maya sutured wounds with human hair, repaired fractures using casts. They were skillful surgeons, made prostheses from Jade and turquoise, and filled teeth with iron pyrite. They used Obsidian blades to perform surgery. Obsidian blades have been used in some U.S. hospitals for heart bypass surgery because they cut cleaner, thereby promoting more rapid healing with less scar tissue. The diseases pinta, leishmaniasis, and yellow fever, and several *psychiatric* syndromes were diagnosed and treated. Even athletes' foot and diarrhea were cured with herbal medicine.

The ancient Maya considered health as "balance," illness and disease were "imbalance." Balance, however, had many factors, such as the season and varied with age, gender, personality, and exposure to environmental temperature extremes. A central medical-related theme held that balance was effected favorably or adversely by *diet!* A key Edgar Cayce concept too! And one that many of us today have come to know as key to health.

The Maya used several plants, such as the Chaya (*Cnidoscolus chayamansa*), also known as Mayan spinach, because of its high content of protein, calcium, iron, and vitamins. They also used the resin of the Ek' Balam shrub, (*Croton flavens L.*), which rapidly seals damaged blood vessel. To treat and close wounds in muscular tissue the bark of the bakalche' tree (*Bourreria pulchra Millsp.*) was applied. This is documented in inscriptions in Quiriguá, Ceibal, Tikal, and *Altar de Sacrificios*, among others. They used Jade also. In fact the name Jade is derived from the Spanish "Piedra de Ijada", *loin-stone,* Jade having been recognized by the Maya as a remedy for kidney ailments – because of its beneficial effect on the kidneys, the stone was also known as "Lapis Nephriticus."

Upper left is Mayan spinach, upper right is Ek' Balam shrub (bitter), and lower left is the bakalche' tree with its healing bark. Lower right is jade stone with Mayan carving. All are indigenous to Mesoamerica.

Legends and Tales of Our Soul's Journey

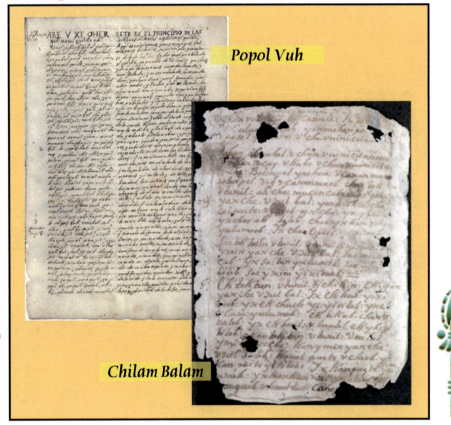

Our study begins at the beginning, the *Genesis* as seen by the Mesoamericans. Their story of how it all began is found in their *Popol Vuh* ("Chronicles of the People" by the Quiché Maya) and the *Chilam Balam* (the book of the "Jaguar Priest" by the Yucatec Maya).

The content of the *Popol Vuh* (pronounced *pope-ul voo*) dates to roughly 1000 to 1500 AD. Therefore it is before the Spanish invasion and conquest. However, this text was copied by Spanish Friar Francisco Ximénez (Jiménez) in the 1700s, he was working from the original text that had been found in the Guatemalan Highlands, somewhere around 1550 and thought to have been authored by Quiché royalty. The *Popol Vuh* is the Quiché Mayan creation story told with much hidden meaning and symbolism.

Above is the title page of the *Popol Vuh* manuscript.
Below is wall carving in El Mirador, Guatemala, of the story dating to *300 BC!*
Archaeologist Richard Hansen is seen in this photo.

One of the fascinating parts of the Mayan creation story is the similarity it shares with the Bible's account of creation and the flood in Genesis, chapters 1-9.

Father Ximénez's manuscript contains the oldest known text of *Popol Vuh*.
It is written in parallel Quiché and Spanish. Below we see the 3 languages.

Quiché: ARE V XE OHER Tzih varal Quiche vbi. Varal xchicatzibah vi xchicatiquiba vi oher tzih, vticaribal, vxenabal puch ronohel xban, pa tinamit quiche, ramac quiche vinac;	**Spanish:** ESTE ES EL PRINCIPIO DE LAS Antiguas historias aqui en el quiche. Aquí escribiremos y empezaremos las Antiguas historias, su principio, y comienzo de todo lo que fue hecho en el pueblo de el quiche, su pueblo de los indios quiches;	**English:** THIS IS THE BEGINNING of the old traditions of this place called Quiché. Here we shall write and we shall begin the old stories, the beginning and the origin of all that was done in the town of the Quiché, by the tribes of the Quiché nation.

Here is a sample of the original text:

Part I, Chapter I

"This is the account of how all was in suspension, all calm, in silence; all motionless, still, and the expanse of the sky was empty.

"First, there was silence, all was in suspension, motionless.

"There was only darkness and empty sky.

"Then there was the Creator(s). [in the Genesis God was named *Elohim*, which is also plural – I believe this to mean all-inclusive oneness]

"Then there were those that conceive and give birth.

"Next came the Word (we also find "the Word" in the Gospel of John, in the original Greek it is actually, the Logos).

"Next came three aspects of the Heart of Heaven, the Trinity. This is the account of how all was in suspension, all calm, in silence; all motionless, still, and the expanse of the sky was empty.

"The Creator brought forth the Great Mother (*Alom*) and the Great Father (*Qahalom*). The Great Mother conceives everything. The Great Father gives breath (spirit) and life (motion) to that conceived.

"This is the first account, the first narrative. There was neither man, nor animal, birds, fishes, crabs, trees, stones, caves, ravines, grasses, nor forests; there was only the sky.

"The surface of the earth had not appeared. There was only the calm sea and the great expanse of the sky.

"There was nothing brought together, nothing which could make a noise, nor anything which might move, or tremble, or could make noise in the sky.

"There was nothing standing; only the calm water, the placid sea, alone and tranquil. Nothing existed.

"There was only immobility and silence in the darkness, in the night. Only the Creator, the Maker, *Tepeu* and *Gucumatz* [in Yucatec this name was *Kukulkan*, in Aztec is was *QuetzalCoatl*], those who conceive and give birth, were in the water surrounded with light. They [this plural nature of the Creator fits with Elohim in Genesis also being plural] were hidden under green and blue feathers, and were therefore called Gucumatz [meaning "Feathered Serpent" or "Plumed Serpent" – as is found in ancient Egyptian lore also, though usually a *winged* serpent]. By nature they were great sages and great thinkers. In this manner the sky existed and also the Heart of Heaven, which is the name of God and thus He is called.

"Then came the word [logos]. Tepeu [the Sovereign or Maker] and Gucumatz [bird-serpent, or mind and life force] came together in the darkness, in the night, and the Maker and the Life Force talked together. They talked, discussing and deliberating; they agreed, they united their words and their thoughts.

"Then while they meditated [ooo, how right-on is this], it became clear to them that when dawn would break, the human must appear. Then they planned the creation, and the growth of the trees and the thickets and the birth of life and the creation of human. Thus it was arranged in the darkness and in the night by the Heart of Heaven who is called "Storm of Creation" (Huracán) [the Big Bang?].

"The first is called "Lightning" (Caculhá Huracán), [in physics: the "Electromagnetic Force"]. The second is "Small Flash" (Chipi-Caculhá), [in physics: the "Weak Force"]. The third is "Green Flash" (Raxa-Caculhá), [in physics: "Strong Force"]. And these three are the Heart of Heaven.

"Then the Maker and the Life Force came together; then they conferred about life and light, what they would do so that there would be light and dawn, who it would be who would provide food and sustenance.

"Thus let it be done! Let the emptiness be filled! Let the water recede and make a void, let the earth appear and become solid; let it be done. Thus they spoke. 'Let there be light, let there be dawn in the sky and on the earth! There shall be neither glory nor grandeur in our creation and formation until the human being is made, human is formed.' So they spoke.

"Then the earth was created by them. So it was, in truth, that they created the earth. 'Earth!' they said, and instantly it was made.

"Like the mist, like a cloud, and like a cloud of dust was the creation, when the mountains appeared from the water; and instantly the mountains grew.

"Only by a miracle, only by magic art were the mountains and valleys formed; and instantly the groves of cypresses and pines put forth shoots together on the surface of the earth.

"And thus Mind/LifeForce was filled with joy, and exclaimed: 'Your coming has been fruitful, Heart of Heaven; and you, Stormy Creation, and you, the Forces of the Creation!'

"'Our work, our creation shall be finished,' they answered.

"First the earth was formed, the mountains and the valleys; the currents of water were divided, the rivulets were running freely between the hills, and the water was separated when the high mountains appeared.

"Thus was the earth created, when it was formed by the Heart of Heaven, the Heart of Earth, as they are called who first made it fruitful, when the sky was in suspension, and the earth was submerged in the water.

"So it was that they made perfect the work, when they did it after thinking and meditating upon it." -END

Here are the two icons of consciousness and energy, as in kundalini.

Quetzal Bird (bird of paradise) and Coatl (feathered serpent)

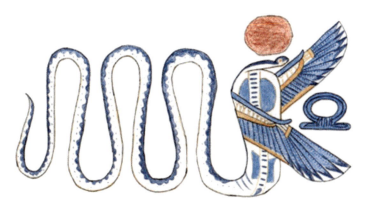

Egyptian *winged* serpent

Quetzalcoatl

    Quetzalcoatl (literally, *bird-serpent*); pronounced *ketzel-co-aat-el*), is a representation and personalization of *each* soul as well as the god who teaches souls. Each soul has lessons and tests in a learning process toward mastering its free will and independent consciousness. And each has to find redemption from damaging mistakes. Every soul must meet the challenge of the battle between self-seeking, self-gratifying use of its will and its godly destiny to be a co-creator and companion with all life and with the great Creator of all life. The "bird" symbolizes the mind and the "serpent" symbolizes the energy or life force within us. In the legends of the Bird-Serpent god – and us as godlings experiencing similar challenges – Quetzalcoatl is a wonder-filled spiritual being of great light and love. It is the "Logos," the Word. This god is associated with Venus, the bright morning star *and* the dark evening star for 260 days. The following provides some insight into this legend:

Venus vs Mars
Struggle between the Light & the Dark

There is a dark side to Quetzalcoatl that he was not aware of or ignored, and that was his "twin" *Xolotl* (pronounced *sho-lot-el*, a deformed dog-like god) and a challenger called Tezcatlipoca (pronounced *tez-cat-lee-po-cah*).

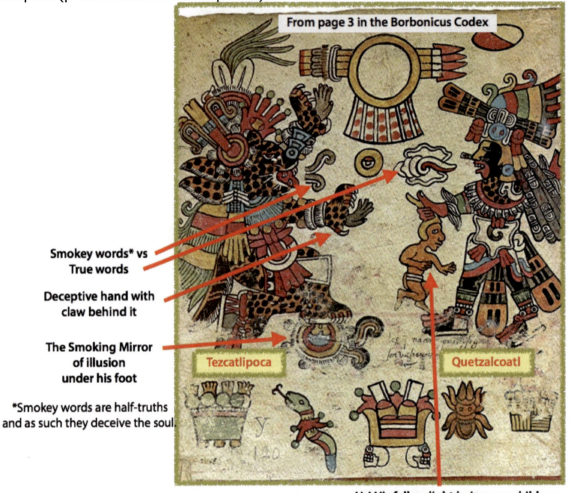

Quetzalcoatl is Venus when it is the bright morning star for 260 days of the year. Xolotl is Venus when it is the dim evening star for 260 days. In Jungian psychology, this would be Quetzalcoatl's *shadow*, which must be addressed and tamed by a higher ideal than unguided, animalistic urges. Quetzalcoatl's dark-side got its day as the legend tells of a time when Quetzalcoatl – and us as godlings – fell from original grace and lost sight of our ultimate destiny as we experienced our dark side. The legend tells how the original light of love was confused and misled by a "Lord of Darkness" named, *Tezcatlipoca*. This Dark Lord is "madness" and Mars and carries a magical, smoking, black mirror of polished obsidian – and is a portion of each of us. The dark influence gained access to the Bird-Serpent's temple-palace (our minds), and once inside began to play on our vanity and confusing us with mirrors (in Mesoamerica mirrors are Venus' weakness for vanity and self-deception).

But, the mirrors only showed our mortality and lower, selfish nature, which upset us. Then we covered this dark side up with decorations – decorations that also hid our truer, deeper, divine nature, leaving us with only the outer self. This caused Quetzalcoatl to party without a higher sense of purpose, resulting in him getting drunk on self indulgence and selfish gratification. On one occasion the bright and wonderful light-being made a fatal mistake by having illicit sex with his sister during a drunken party. The next morning Quetzalcoatl rose dimmed and in shock and dishonor – to himself and those around him. Due to the loss of his control over his urges and passions, he fell from grace. The Aztecs held to a prophecy that he would rise again and return to his original brightness – divine again and much wiser (symbolized by the return of Venus as the morning star after enduring 260 days as the dark *night-time* star).

In these two illustrations we see how the energy of the Life Force, symbolized by the feathered serpent (Quetzalcoatl) can rise to give strength to us (first image) – or it can overwhelm us and we lose our heads (second image). The Life Forces can be misused by ego, self-exaltation, will-fullness, and impulsive selfishness. How do we handle this? We set a higher ideal than selfishness. The higher ideal of our better self motivates and guides us, not allowing the darker side of our egocentric self and its pursuits to rule us? This is the proverbial battle between good and evil, light and dark, life and death – a common theme in Mesoamerican stories as well as most ancient legends. (Note: In the first image above notice the bowl from which our better self rises, in the bowl are papers blotted with our blood, symbolizing our sacrificing selfishness for a higher purpose.)

The Chilam Balam

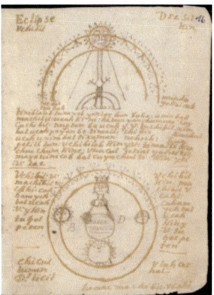

    The *Chilam Balam* is a Yucatec Mayan text. There are 9 known books, all handwritten. The Mani version of the *Chilam Balam* bears the following title: *U than hahal ku tu nathob Chilam*, which could be translated: "The words of the true God which Chilam understood." The introduction states that the other great Maya prophets assembled at the house of the Jaguar Priest. Chilam Balam (literally, "Jaguar Priest") lay stretched out in a trance in his room, during which he received a revelation which descended from above, and which only he understood. Eventually these revelations were written down, see illustrations above. This is reminiscent of John's Revelation in the Bible, which he received during a trance-like state while seeking God's guidance.

    The 9 books date back to the time of the Spanish invasion and conquest, however they contain content from ancient times. The text include chronicles, prophecies, rituals, and even medical practices. In addition to these two major documents there are also "codices" containing information and images that add to our knowledge of Mesoamerican perspectives on life and death and after-life.

Mayan Codices

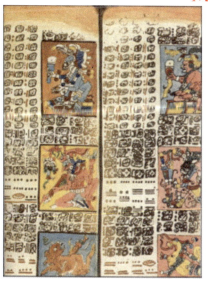

Dresden Codex　　　　　　Madrid Codex

A Folded Codex

    The codices fold like an accordion. They are actually screen-folds of long strips of deer hide, cotton cloth or bark paper (usually from a fig tree), occasionally protected by wooden covers. Each page is divided into either horizontal or vertical bands separated by bright red lines, and is read in a back-and-forth fashion, alternating lines one way then the other way. Of the Mayan codices, only four survive today, and are named by the location that possesses them: Dresden, Madrid, Paris, and Grolier. But some two dozen codices of other Mesoamerican groups still exist. The largest group of early codices are early Mixtec pictographic books from Oaxaca (pronounced, *wah-hak-kah*), Mexico. We will also study images and tales from various temple complex in addition to these texts.

Stories and Dates on Stelae (Steles)

Stone pillars and free-standing slabs containing inscriptions of significant people, events, and dates.

A Mayan Stele is a Record on Stone

Fallen Stele in the Jungle of Guatemala at Piedras Negras

The Story of the Twins and Xquic (*she-queek*)

You need to read this as an *allegorical story* representing portions
of our soul-being engaged in a struggle with good and evil,
light and dark, soul growth and death.

This warrior ballplayer wearing the Jaguar helmet will act as our guide.

The Legend goes like this:

At the beginning of the Third Creation, "Grandfather of the Light" as the Sun and "Grandmother of the Light" as the Moon, made love together. They were not the physical Sun and Moon but the *essence* of these Lights. Through their love making they conceived the *Maize-God Twins*, named One Maize "Ear" (of corn) and Seven Maize "Seeds" (corn kernels). They represent our mind and seven chakras – like seven rays of the white light through the prism of individualness. These were the spirit of the life force coming into Matter, a life force that could sustain a physical body. As we became more physical (but not as physical as we are today), the names changed. The two Maize Gods were now called "One Hunter Lord" and "Seven Hunter Lord." The term "Hunter" indicatied our motivation to seek out dark forces with our blowguns (a symbol of the power of breath or *prana* over death and darkness).

One of the Maize Gods using blowgun to take down a lord of the Underworld.

These Maize-God Twins played ball often and dressed in the finest and most elaborate ball-playing gear.

One Hunter married "She of Fastened Bones," indicating another step deeper into physicality and Matter. She gave birth to the Monkey Twins: "One Howler Monkey" and "One Spider Monkey." Unlike their father and uncle, the Monkey Twins were very productive in many aspects of life beyond playing ballgames. They were very clever. And they were skilled in painting, sculpting, and blow-gunning. They were learning and growing in many directions – becoming well-rounded.

This part of the story reveals the difference between the Maize-God Twins and the Monkey Twins. In most mystical teachings these two sets of twins symbolize the difference between *mind* and *will*; mind may have knowledge but *will* is knowledge *applied*. The Maize-God Twins just play ball. The Monkey Twins grow and contribute.

In the story the Monkey Twins would often play exciting ball games against their father and uncle (the Maize-God Twins). The Dark Lords of the "Hidden World" or "Unseen World," the *Underworld* (called, "Xibalba," pronounced *she-bal-ba*, meaning "fearful place" and "place of phantoms"), coveted the amazing ball-playing *gear* of the Maize-God Twins. The Dark Lords were also upset by all the noise and commotion resulting from the ball games being played on their heads (they lived underground). Therefore, the Lords of the Underworld sent two owls up to the surface to invite the Maize-God Twins to come into the Underworld for a game with the Dark Lords. The Dark Lords required that the Maize-God Twins bring all of their marvelous gear with them (hint, hint).

The Maize God Twins in their ballgame uniforms

There are 12 Lords of the Underworld; the two leading Dark Lords are "One Death" and "Seven Death" (symbolizing the selfish mind and the seven chakras used for self-gratification and self-glorification). One Death and Seven Death bring death, while the remaining 10 Dark Lords have domain over various forms of human suffering: sickness, starvation, fear, destitution, pain, and various forms of dying. The Underworld is also filled with fallen souls who are now under the dominion of one of these Dark Lords, and cannot get free without help from above.

The Maize-God Twins descend into the darkness of the subterranean Underworld, crossing violent rivers and thorn bushes. Finally they cross the "River of Blood," descending deeper and deeper into physicality and lonesome self (more on this later). They come to a four-way crossroads of colors: Red, Black, White, and Yellow. The Black Road spoke to them, saying, "I am the way of the Lord." And they took that path.

This legend is about the beginning of our learning, and so we made several mistakes before finally gaining understanding and mastery over our impulses. And as Edgar Cayce taught, we are to *do* something, right or wrong, make a choice, because in the *doing* comes the understanding. It is not in the hearing or reading, but in actually engaging life! This leads to understanding and enlightenment.

Though the Maize-God Twins were gods, they were naive and immature. They did not know deception, lies, false-fronts, and hypocrisy. As a result, the Dark Lords of the Underworld played many tricks on them, and the Lords laughed and laughed at the Twins' confusion and mistakes. They laughed so hard that their bellies hurt. Then the Dark Lords invited the Twins to enter a house (a state of consciousness and emotion). This house was the "House of Gloom." If the Twins could make it through the night, then the Dark Lords would play the ball game tomorrow, and by doing so risk defeat. There was one catch, the Lords gave the Twins some "smokes" and "pine sticks" (matches) to light their pipes, but warned the Twins that they had to have some left come morning or they would suffer the consequences.

The House of Gloom was very dark and dank, and the night was long and moonless.

When morning came the Twins had used up all of the smokes and pine sticks. For this failure the Dark Lords "killed" them, and put One Hunter's head on a Calabash tree as a sign of the Dark Lords' prowess. But, to everyone's surprise, when they put the head on the tree, the tree burst forth with the most amazing fruit! This was so confounding that the seeming victory over the Twins was diminished. Out of concern for their control, One Death and Seven Death instructed everyone in the Underworld to never, ever approach the tree. If they did, the penalty would be death by cutting their heart out.

Xquic (*she-queek*), the virgin daughter of a Dark Lord, heard this story of the Maize-God's head hanging on a tree in the "Place of Sacrifices." Her father had told her the story. When the "Blood Maiden" heard the story of the fruit on that tree, she wanted to see it and taste it. She asked, "Why can I not go to see this tree which they tell about? Surely the fruit of which I hear tell must be very good." Her father told her of the curse, but she went alone and arrived at the foot of the tree planted in the "Place of Sacrifices."

"Ah!" she exclaimed. "What fruit is this that this tree bears? Is it not wonderful to see how it is covered with fruit? Must I die, shall I be lost, if I pick one of this fruit?" asked the virgin daughter of the Dark Lord. Then the Maize-God's skull which was among the branches of the tree spoke up and said: "What is it you wish? Those round objects that cover the branches of the trees are nothing but skulls." So spoke the head of the Maize-God Twin, One Hunter.

Then, to the maiden the head said,
"Do you, perchance, want them?"
"Yes, I want them," the maiden answered.
"Very well," said the skull. "Stretch your hand up here."
"Very well," said the maiden, and with her hand she reached toward the skull.

In that instant the skull let drops of spittle fall directly into the maiden's palm. She looked quickly and intently at the palm of her hand, but the spittle of the skull was not there!

Then the skull said, "In my saliva and spittle I have given you my descendants. Now my head has nothing on it any more, it is nothing but a skull without life. So are the heads of the great princes, the flesh is all that gives them a handsome appearance. And when they die, men are frightened by their bones. The nature of the sons of a lord, of a wise man, or of an orator, which are like saliva and spittle, do not lose their substance when they go, but they *bequeath* it. The nature of the lord, of the wise man, or of the orator does not disappear, nor is it lost, but he leaves it to the daughters and to the sons which he begets. I have done the same with you. Go up, then, to the surface of the earth, that you may not die. Believe in my words that it will be so." Thus spoke the head the Maize-God Twin.

Now, all that Xquic and the Maize-God did together was by order of the "Heart of Heaven."

Credit: Artist Wayne Ferrebee

After this conversation, the maiden returned directly to her home, having immediately conceived the sons in her belly by virtue of the spittle. And thus the coming *Hero Twins* were conceived. And so the girl returned home, and after six months had passed the maiden's secret was discovered by her father when he observed that she was pregnant. The punishment was to have her heart cut out and burned in the fire. Four owls were to escort her to a distant place, cut out her heart, and then bring it to the Lords of the Underworld to burn. When they arrived at the place for the sacrifice, she said to the owls: "It cannot be that you will kill me, oh, messengers, because what I bear in my belly is no disgrace, but was begotten when I went to marvel at the head of the Maize-God Twin. So, then, you must not sacrifice me, oh, messengers!"

The owls replied, "And what shall we put in place of your heart? Your father told us: 'Bring the heart, return before the lords, do your duty, all working together, bring it in the gourd quickly, and put the heart in the bottom of the gourd.' Perchance, did he not speak to us so? What shall we put in the gourd? We wish too, that you should not die."

"Very well, but my heart does not belong to them. Neither is your home here, nor must you let them force you to kill me. Later, in truth, the real criminals will be at your mercy and I will overcome One Death and Seven Death. So, then, the blood and only the blood shall be theirs and shall be given to them. Neither shall my heart be burned before them. Gather the produce of this tree," instructed the maiden. The red sap gushing forth from the tree fell in the gourd and with it they made a ball which glistened and took the shape of a heart. The tree gave forth sap similar to blood, with the appearance of real blood. Then the blood, or that is to say the sap of the red tree, clotted, and formed a very bright coating inside the gourd, like clotted blood; meanwhile the tree glowed at the work of the maiden. It was called the "red tree of cochineal," [a cactus that yields red dye] but since then it has taken the name of Blood Tree because its sap is called Blood. [Clearly we're shifting from blood to sap, as Jesus did to wine, and an actual physical heart to a symbolic heart.]

"There on earth you shall be beloved and you shall have all that belongs to you," said the maiden to the owls.

"Very well, girl. We shall go there, we go up to serve you; you, continue on your way, while we go to present the sap, instead of your heart, to the lords," said the messengers.

The maiden ascended out of the dark and gave birth to a new set of twins –
the Hero Twins. She was surprised that their earth family was not accepting of these new twins. She asked, "Did they not know that these were to become the conquerors of the Lords of the Underworld, avengers of the Maize-God Twins' deaths?"

However, she had to understand that the Hero Twins were partly the seed of the Underworld and their mother was a daughter of that dark world. It didn't matter that her heart did not belong to the Underworld, she was not of the earthy surface family.

Strangely, despite how the Hero Twins were being treated by their family, they held no anger or bitterness. In fact, the Hero Twins held no negative thoughts toward anyone! Their minds were clear and their hearts were calm. However, they did possessed the *fearlessness* of their maiden mother – for she entered the Place of Sacrifices alone and against the curse of the Dark Lords. This would prove to be their most powerful asset when they eventually faced the Dark Lords in the Place of Fear and Phantoms (*Xibalba*). Unlike the Maize-God Twins, their father and uncle, the Hero Twins were never tricked by the Dark Lords, thus there was no laughter shared by the Dark Lords, only concern and wonderment. After all the tests, including the night in the House of Gloom, the Hero Twins overcame every test in the darkness and deaths. They knew deep within themselves that this was all an illusion, an illusion designed to create confusion, doubt, and fear. Using quiet, enduring faith, some magic, and much cleverness the Hero Twins caused One Death and Seven Death to be no more.

Throughout history the feminine has played major roles in keeping the light on and spiritual growth progressing. Here is a brief Bible list of key women: Lilith, Eve, Rachel, Rebecca, Hannah, Esther, Mary, and the Divine Feminine in Chapter 12 of the Revelation. in Mayan, Toltec, Aztec lore we find the same: Xmucané, Ix'Chel (Moon goddess), Xbaquiyalo, Xquic ... and many more.

In Mesoamerican lore, especially Mayan, the feminine and masculine are always paired together. There is no masculine without the feminine. For example, the first humans are pairs, male & female: *Balam Quitze* & *Choim'ha*, meaning "Sweet smiling Jaguar" & "Beautiful Water" and *Balam Akab* & *Kaha-Paluma*, meaning "Night Jaguar" & "Falling Water".

Now you may think that the Maya want each of us to have opposite gender companions, and at the earth level this would be the natural way, but these male and female expressions are aspects *inside one whole entity*, one soul. And as we have been doing for many years now, each of us needs to get in touch with his or her *inner compliment* to the outer gender. In this way our consciousness becomes whole and our vibrations harmonious. Yin and Yang are one. And as you can see in this yin-yang symbol, there's a little yin in the yang and a little yang in the yin. A whole soul contains both dynamics, even though it only projects one. The feminine is the deeper, intuitive portion of oneself, the womb of life who can bring nourishment from within herself through her breasts to feed new life. The masculine is external aspect of one's being, carrier of the sword, tiller of the soil, and symbolizes outer strength for physical action and victory. The two work together.

In this story the womb of consciousness (Xquic) conceives new powers via the water of life from what appears to be dead (spittle from the Maize god). The owls of wise thinking perceive the greater truth about the situation, and do not let the darkness have their way with this new life. The new life is wiser and purer of heart and mind, thereby overcoming all the illusions of power and darkness. It is a tale for every soul.

Our Soul Story in the San Bartolo Mural

In Guatemala, near the famous site of Tikal, there is a captivating Mayan masterpiece painted inside a temple pyramid. It is known as the "San Bartolo Mural." Actually there are two murals but we are going to focus on the north wall (circa 300 BC). Illustration #1 is a panorama of what remains of this interesting mural. The other illustrations highlight stages along this intriguing story, filled so beautiful with imagery and symbolism.

A reconstruction of this faded mural was made in 2007 by archaeologist and archaeological illustrator Heather Hurst, and is on display at the site.

Rebirth!

There are two scenes on the north wall: the first scene flows from right to left on a path that leads to the second scene of a soaring climax of rebirth! (Notice the babies with their umbilical cords in the square image on this page) The path leads to a symbolic Tree of Life filled with vitality and abundance. The whole mural may be seen as a Mayan version of the Revelation – a revelation about the life of our earthly selves, our souls, and the forces – both seen and unseen – that help us conceive in our hearts and minds a truth sufficient to birth our immortal selves! And since our earthly self is temporary, living until the body fails, it is important to conceive and birth our after-death self – and this can be done long before the death of our body.

Now let's go to the path (next page). Notice the footprints indicating that we walk this path. Also notice that there are three color levels under our feet: red, yellowish color, and white. These likely symbolize our three levels of existence: in the blood body (red), in the personality-ego self (daytime-like yellowish color), and in the higher soul-self (white level), see illustration #2 on the next page.

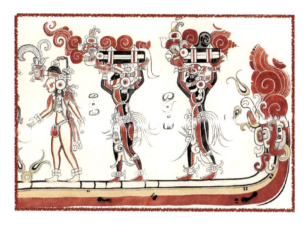
Illustration #2

As you can see the images convey a mystical, metaphysical view of life, seeing us as souls who are only temporarily living physically and are gradually being forced to live as spirit-minds beyond this world. It is the path that our outer and inner self travel in order to awaken and birth that portion of us that God conceived when it was said: "Let there be Light!" That was the light of consciousness, consciousness at a soul level. Cayce's readings teach: "The Spirit moved… and there was Light – Mind. The Light became the light of humanity – Mind made aware of conscious existence in spiritual … relationships as one to another. The mind in the entity becomes aware of longings, innate in the inner self; also the arousing of emotions in the physical attributes of the body…. Self is a part of Creative Forces or God, Spirit, the Son. These are one. The body, mind, and soul are one. Their desires must be one; their purposes, their aims must be one – to be ideal." (1947-3)

And in the San Bartolo mural we see the Maya's wonderful depiction of our life path, leading to this all-important rebirth. Using symbols, they show how the journey has stages with powerful and profound transitions. The whole mural portrays the majestic flow of life's journey as a great river inescapably flows to the sea, a sea of oneness again.

Our original birth was not the birth of the physical self or even physical body. It was the birth of our spirit and mind. But we lost awareness of this. And as we have become increasingly alone in one body, our outer selves appear to be all we are. However, there was a time – so very long ago – when we sang as members of the "Morning Stars," referring to the biblical book of Job 38:7. Back then we were all together in oneness with the Spirit, moving as would a flock of birds turning in unison or a school of fish swimming to and fro in a harmonious pattern. We never felt alone, but always in an oneness with all life. In our present condition we all appear to be separated, so we must awaken once again to the oneness and rebirth our Morning-Star self. Cayce said that biblical Adam was not just an individual but also a soul group, and we (our souls) were members of that group. (900-227)

Let's interpret the images in this strange and wonderful mural. On the next few pages we'll see a perspective that is beyond the physical beauty of this mural – a perspective that may help us open to the intentions of the original painters of this mural.

Illustration #3

Here we see our individualized soul-self represented as the divine feminine with two symbols of enlightenment: her crown-chakra topknot and her forehead owl of wisdom (her third eye – owls have exceptional vision and are a totem for wisdom). The little red circle before her nose symbolizes the Breath of Life that she now breathes (as revealed in Genesis, chapter 2). She is venturing toward rebirthing her truer self. Notice the two beings following her in illustration #2 on the previous page; they are carrying treasures on their heads. The treasures on their heads symbolize the influences of their minds' understanding and wisdom. Cayce identifies the "two witnesses" in the Revelation as our *conscious* and *subconscious* minds bringing testimony of our spiritual mind's existence. (281-33) The black-colored portions of the Mayan "witnesses" symbolize the *unseen* influences and the red portions the *seen*. Notice also how the path begins with reddish energies descending from above and then flowing along the pathway, always underfoot, always influencing our *under*standing.

Illustration #4

Next, we see two beings, one above the other. The lower flesh-colored one is feminine and the upper red one is masculine, the yin and yang of our whole being. Interestingly, "adam" in Hebrew means, "reddish being," owing to the blood in the body. And in many ancient cultures the feminine was always painted in soft, pale tones because she is the "fairer sex." These two beings are in the pose of *supplication* to the life-giving Maize god (illustration #6 on the next page). They cause the powerful god to turn his head to them, and that swirling red antenna-like projection coming from his mouth may be his message or his energy flowing to them. In front of the Maize god's body and arms is a kneeling black-colored being, indicating an unseen being (black indicating hidden, unseen, and dark, but not evil). The Maize god is helping him birth a calabash gourd from out of his crown chakra. Notice the Mayan symbol on this gourd (looks like a white U in the yellow band); it is the glyph for *emergence*, and as such may also mean *birth*. Illustration #5 means "emergence." Notice the gourd's umbilical-like vine extending upward to the heavens, or having a connection to the heavens and receiving life-support from the heavens, as a mother's umbilicus gives life to a fetus. This gourd is the womb in which the gestation occurs. It is the womb from which will emerge the new consciousness, the new life—making us more a soul with a mind than a body with a personality. This womb abides in our higher consciousness, as indicated by the crown chakra location from which it emerges.

Illustration #5   Illustration #6

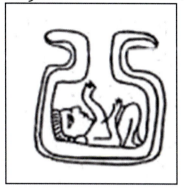

Illustration #5 is "birth" or "emergence"

Illustration #6 is a red-colored being and a black-colored being with gourde on his head with a U symbol on the gourd. The red being is the Maize God, with his head turned toward the worshipping yin and yang portion of our being in Illustration #4.

Below is a kneeling female offering nourishment to those attempting this birth. Behind and above her is the Mayan version of the Tree of Life, stylized. Their Tree contains not only the infamous serpent of the Garden of Eden but also the jaguar and the lizard. And for us to understand this we must first understand what a *totem* is to these ancient people. A totem is an image of an animal believed to have spiritual significance and is used as an *emblem* reflecting that animal's special powers. For the Maya, the jaguar symbolizes the ability to live in the two worlds: the outer world of the day (this world, this life) and the inner world of the night (the mind-spirit world, the inner life). They knew that the jaguar is active both day and night. Add to this that the jaguar will swim through water comfortably, unusual for a cat – symbolizing a power to cross seemingly impossible barriers. Our impossible barrier and passage from this reality to the mind-spirit reality gives the jaguar a special place of honor in our totem of helpful influences in the Tree of Life.

The Maya also considered the lizard to symbolize how the lowliness of physical life may produce a wondrous being of high mindedness and purpose, for in Mayan lore the lizard was initially one of the *creation gods*, one who helped make an early prototype of human beings. Unfortunately, the lizard god later became so envious of the humans that he broke many rules and was cursed to live in the mud among the first humans, who were mindless and heartless. However, from this world's mud was born improved human beings! They became the children of the Maize god. They were tall, strong, and wise men and women, known as the *Blue Maize People.* The mud's magical ability to awaken the spark of life that is *latent* within corn seeds, thus bringing forth the life-sustaining plant could also magically cause muddy humans to emerge anew. All of this is showing us how we too may burst forth from the mud of our life to a new, better life. Edgar Cayce noted that, "From some of the ugliest swamps come some of the most beautiful lilies!"

Now as for the serpent in the Mayan Tree of Life, most ancient cultures considered the serpent to symbolize the *life force* within the body that lies mostly in the lower chakras but may be raised to higher levels by the wings of the mind when the entity dwells on higher, more metaphysical thoughts. Thus, the winged-serpent was a revered image, totem, and icon.

Even modern medical professionals wear the *caduceus*, which has two serpents rising up with wings above them. The savior god of the Maya was *Kukulkán* (Yucatan Maya) and *Gucumatz* (Quiché Maya), and as we've learned, both of these names may be translated as *featured serpent*. Raising the Life Force to higher vibrations was a major teaching in ancient cultures, and we find the same with the Maya. Part of our spiritual path is raising our vibrations – as was sung in the 1960s song by the Beach Boys, "Good Vibrations." In the '60s we were more aware of people's vibes, which led us to avoid some and drawn to others. This is depicted in the medical professions caduceus (left) for healing and health – when the life forces of the body are at higher vibrations health results.

If you look closely at the Tree of Life on page 43, you'll also see birds gathering seed from a bag hanging on the Tree – a symbol of our higher thoughts (birds) continuing to gather nourishing seeds of truth from the Tree of Life. This is very reminiscent of Kabbalah's Tree of Life with its ten emanations of God that enliven us and awaken us to our spiritual nature. And Jesus used "birds of the air" as a symbol of God's awareness of all life, including ours. Cayce taught: "That you are alive, that you are conscious, and that you have the opportunity in this period to apply self in the reconstruction of what man is to look forward to, should encourage you to know that God is mindful of each soul. Then use the abilities that you have, and you have many." (EC 3689-1)

Illustration #7

In this illustration we see a larger gourd upon which the symbol of emergence is inscribed: U. The first gourd, coming out of the head of the black-colored being (#6) may

be the *microcosmic* or individual experience of rebirth. This large, second gourd may represent the *macrocosmic* or *soul group* experience of rebirth. Notice the four babies with umbilical cords surrounding a fifth entity emerging directly out of the gourd with a white bandana around his head. According to Cayce's numerology five is the number of a human being – having five senses, five appendages (1 head, 2 arms, 2 legs), and five races. And in Kabbalah five is the number of humans who have subdued their earthy nature. Standing next to this exploding birth scene is a being that may well symbolize our divine self with its astonishing consciousness indicated by the massive and wondrous headdress. Notice the serpent-energy is raised and emerging from a feathered icon atop his head, and in the serpent's mouth is a string with a tiny face and a third-eye. This may indicate the delicate nature of our spiritual self in the midst of earthly interests, urges, and influences. Notice also that our higher self is wearing armor! And notice the symbol for emergence in several locations on this armor. The armor may indicate our ultimate mastery over earthly and egotistical illusions, and that we have battled against the negative energies *and won!*

These ideas of a necessary spiritual birth – so beautifully depicted in this mural – are not new and do not belong solely to the Maya. They are found in the wisdom teachings of peoples around the planet. Consider this teaching from the Bible:

"Jesus said to Nicodemus, 'Truly, I say to you, without a new birth no one is able to see the kingdom of God.' Nicodemus said to him, 'How is it possible for a man to be born when he is old? Is he able to go into his mother's womb a second time and come to birth again?' Jesus said in answer, 'Truly, I say to you, if a man's birth is not from water and from the Spirit, it is not possible for him to go into the kingdom of God. That which has been born from the flesh is flesh, and that which has been born from the Spirit is spirit. Do not be surprised that I say to you, it is necessary for you to have a second birth. The wind blows where it pleases, and the sound of it comes to your ears, but you are unable to say from where it comes and to where it goes, so it is with everyone whose birth is from the Spirit.'" (John 3:3-8) The second birth is spiritual.

Whoever painted this mural had a deep understanding into the journey of a soul while incarnate in this world. And they obviously wanted to share this insight and lesson with others – even us today.

A Major Mayan Site in Petén, Guatemala Near Tikal

The wall as it appears today.

Artistic reconstruction by Heather Hurst.

Artist Heather Hurst 2007

Teachings inside Temples & Pyramids
We now begin to Study 4 Major Temple Complexes

A Map of Major Mesoamerican Locations and their Migration from Ancient Lands

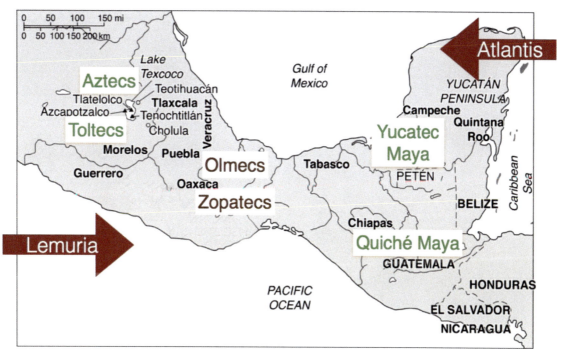

Quiché is pronounced: *KEY-chay*

A Map of 4 Major Mesoamerican Temple Complexes

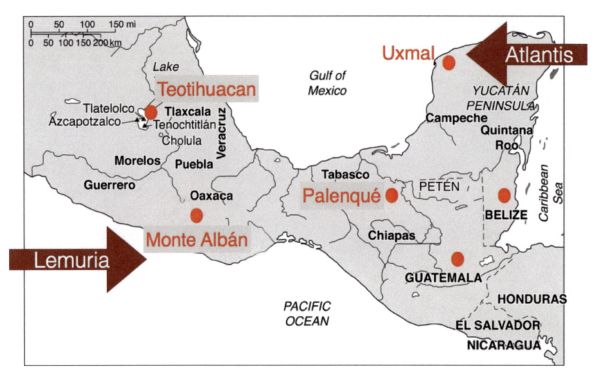

Uxmal is pronounced: *OOSH-mal*
Teotihuacan is pronounced: *tay-o-tee-WA-CON*
Palenqué is pronounced: *pa-LAN-kay*

We are now going through 4 Temple Trainings

Temple 1: Illusions of the Game – Monte Albán Complex

Temple 2: Stages to the Light – Palenqué Complex

Temple 3: Mastering the Forces of Life – Teotihuacán Complex

Temple 4: The Magician Within Us – Uxmal Complex

We are now going to visit these spectacular temple complexes and study the fascinating concepts associated with them and various teachings and trainings.

TEMPLE 1: Illusions of the Game of Life

Monte Albán (Spanish name) or "Sacred Hill of Life"

(600 BC to 750 AD)

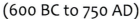

This complex has an array of temples around a central temple, a "holy of holies," is perched on a flatten mountain top. Inside the central temple one can view the rising and setting sun at summer and autumn solstices and the equinoxes. The most unique feature of this site and its people was there *peacefulness!* A succession of Olmecs, Zapotecs, and Mixtecs occupied it. Among a land of warriors the people of Monte Albán maintained a peaceful relationship with their neighbors. The original, native name for this complex was *Danipaguache*, meaning "Sacred Hill of Life." At one time it was surrounded by water on three sides, making it a very dynamic location for sea travel and trade. It is a well-preserved site with many fascinating artifacts and features to impress the modern researcher and tourist visitor. There are over 1,200 monuments on this site. It is located in Oaxaca (pronounced, *wa-ha-ka*), Mexico.

Among the many interesting artifacts on this site are 300 so-called "Dancers," which are stone slabs depicting humans with chakra-like symbols on their bodies.

The Ball Court at Monte Albán

Ball Court at Copan   Ball Court at Coba

More than 1,300 ancient Ball Courts have been found to date.

Playing ball on the ball court was more than a ball game to these people, it was a metaphor for the Game of Life.

To the right are Ballplayers wearing headdress and costumes. This is on a pottery vessel now in the Chrysler Museum.

Ballgame Symbolizing its Ritual Nature

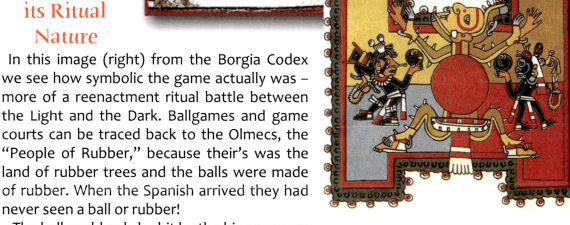

In this image (right) from the Borgia Codex we see how symbolic the game actually was – more of a reenactment ritual battle between the Light and the Dark. Ballgames and game courts can be traced back to the Olmecs, the "People of Rubber," because their's was the land of rubber trees and the balls were made of rubber. When the Spanish arrived they had never seen a ball or rubber!

The ball could only be hit by the hips or upper thighs (no hands or feet) and it had to go into a ring high on the wall of the ball court. See images below.

Shaman Priest Itzamna and 4 keys to Winning the Game of Life.

Itzamna is pronounced, *it-zah-mm-na*. *Itz* means "of the clouds" or "of the heavens." He is referred to as "god D" and considered to be the founder of the Mayan culture and a teacher of his people. We will now learn how to win the game of life by understanding the illusions that handicap us. As in Hinduism's Shiva, the destroyer of illusions, Itzamna helps us overcome our illusions about the forces that challenge us and often defeat us – in preparation for winning the game of life.

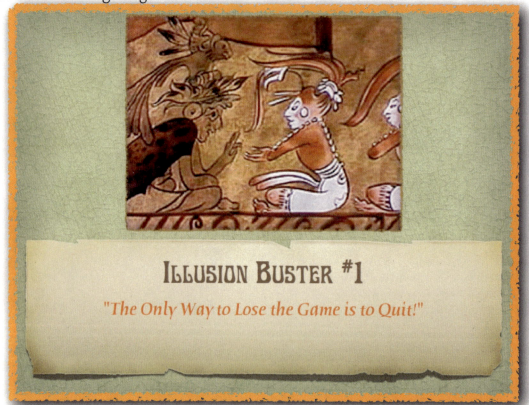

ILLUSION BUSTER #1

"The Only Way to Lose the Game is to Quit!"

There is only one way to lose the game: Stop Playing.

As long as you keep getting up from any loses or disappointments, you continue to have the opportunity to win the game of life (despite how many incarnations or lifetimes it may take our soul!

TIP: Even death is not a game-ender, because our soul never dies.

As Edgar Cayce taught: "Keep on keeping on. Keep on working with, for, toward, the more perfect understanding" (EC 281-9) Adding that there is "no surer way of getting there!"

Illusion Buster #2

"The More You Play, the More You Learn and Improve Your Skill!"

The More You Play, the More You Learn and Improve Your Skill!

The game requires that you face your opponent, come to know him, learn his strengths and weaknesses, and then engage him in a struggle for a higher ideal.

In the Game of Life your opponent lives in the Underworld of your thoughts, emotions, urges, and poor habit patterns. These influences challenge you, often overcome you, and keep you from victory. You must become aware of them, engage them, and ultimately master them.

As God said to Cain who killed Abel, "Sin lies at your door (the door of your consciousness) and its desire is for you. You must master it!" (Genesis 4:7) In Hebrew Cain means *acquired*, referring our growing egos, especially as they grew to become self-centered and selfish. Abel means *breath*, and is our soul-self, given the breath of life to become living souls, as stated in Genesis 2:7, "Lord God formed man from the dust of the ground, and breathed into his nostrils the breath of life; and man became a living soul." The ego kills the soul but God insist that this acquired self will be accepted if it does well, Genesis 4:6-7: "The Lord said to Cain, 'Why are you angry, and why has your countenance fallen? If you do well, will you not be accepted? And if you do not do well, sin is couching at the door; its desire is for you, but you must master it.'"

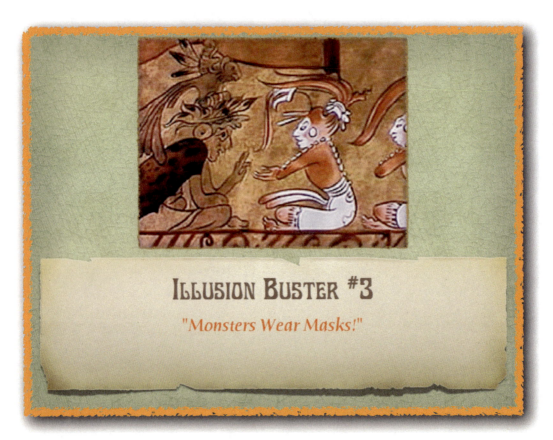

Illusion Buster #3

"Monsters Wear Masks!"

Monsters Wear Masks!

Forces opposing our efforts to become our better self often appear to be monstrous and unbeatable, but this is only their *appearance*, it is not their true nature. Many have faced terrible "beasts" in their lives yet they become victorious. Consider how many alcoholics and drug addicts have overcome these destructive, life-crushing addictions. There are many monstrous challenges in our live that appeared impossible to overcome. But nothing, nothing is as powerful as the will to do so. Often this will needs the strength of higher purpose for overcoming and the help of higher forces.

In the Mayan stories of the Twins, the Hero Twins were victorious over the Dark Lords of the Underworld because they knew the Lords ruled by creating fear and anxiety in their opponents. Xquic, the Blood Maiden, also possessed an inner faith sufficient to avoid fear of the Dark Lords' curse and mindful enough to engage the Owls to understand a greater truth than the Lords' orders to kill her.

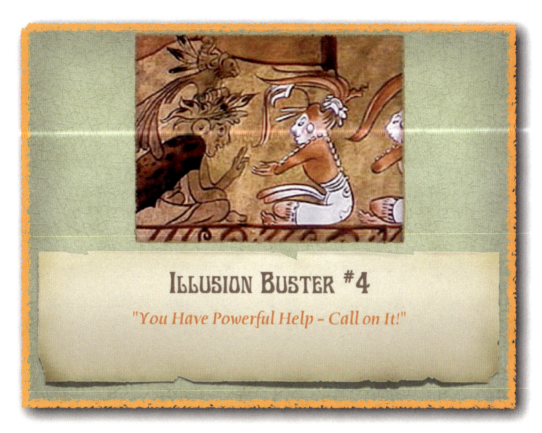

Illusion Buster #4

"You Have Powerful Help - Call on It!"

You Have Powerful Help - Call on It!

The gift of free-willed independence and individual consciousness cannot be taken away. It was given by the Creative Forces of Life. Thus, one must seek help beyond oneself, ask for help beyond oneself, then all the Forces of Life can flow to our aid. Our free will cannot be overrun by any of the great powers, so we must invite, call, evoke these powers to help us!

As Jesus taught: "With men it is impossible, but not with God; for all things are possible with God." (Mark 10:27)

Fear of the challenge and doubt about your abilities are your greatest opponents. Courage, faith, and endurance are your teammates. But it helps to know that you have latent talents and unseen heavenly help available to you. However, you must seek such help, call on the higher and inner forces in order to receive their help.

Edgar Cayce taught: "That you are alive, that you are conscious, and that you have the opportunity in this period to apply self in the reconstruction of what man is to look forward to, should encourage you to know that God is mindful of each soul. Then use the abilities that you have, and you have many." (EC 3689-1) As the creations of the Creator of the entire universe, we do indeed have many abilities – but they are mostly latent within us waiting to be applied in our lives, our struggles and our growth.

Treasures of Wisdom Inside Temples and Chambers

Temple 2: Stages to the Light - Palenqué Temple Complex

Some of the most revealing content about Mesoamerican concepts of soul life are found on the walls of temples and chambers at Palenqué, a beautiful complex in the rainforest.

The Palenqué Complex

Eight rivers flow to this site and the Mayans built an aqueduct to carry water through the site. The complex is located at the end of the Eastern plains, near the Usumacinta River, and just inside the beginning of the Western, mountainous rainforest.

Palenqué is pronounced: *pa-LAN-kay*

Palenqué is built alongside rivers and falls. Archaeologists have discovered remains of 1,500 structures and at least 35 major building complexes on this site.

Here in Palenqué we are going to learn the Mesoamerican understanding of *planes of consciousness* upon which life exists. We may think that we only live in the daily earth plane, but we do not! And this isn't mysticism, it's because we spend 33% of our consciousness and existence ASLEEP! And sleep research centers have mounds of evidence that we are ACTIVE at this deeper plane of consciousness and that it can be as real to us as the outer world!

The Mesoamericans believed that we can traverse these planes of consciousness and existence *while incarnate*, engaging with the heavenly beings as well as the Dark Lords of the Underworld in the ongoing battle for enlightenment.

In the minds of the Mesoamericans there are many forces influencing us, and we need to engage these forces in our journey. These forces are seen and unseen. They are personal and impersonal. They are in the world around us and the world *within* us.

The ancient Maya believed in *recurring cycles of creation and destruction*. They thought in terms of ages lasting about 5,200 modern years. Their recent cycle began in 3114 BC and ended on the Winter Solstice of 2012 AD – more on this later.

They also believed in reincarnation, and wrote of their past lives on walls and stelae. Thus, they believed in progressive development for soul growth. In their legends, the Bird-Serpent god had us all put our hearts into this soul journey, and each star in the heavens is one of the hearts of the Children of God. *One of the stars above is yours!*

Of Interest to our Study are 3 Temples on this Complex
There are Fascinating Tablets inside these 3 Temples
Let's explore them for insight and meaning...

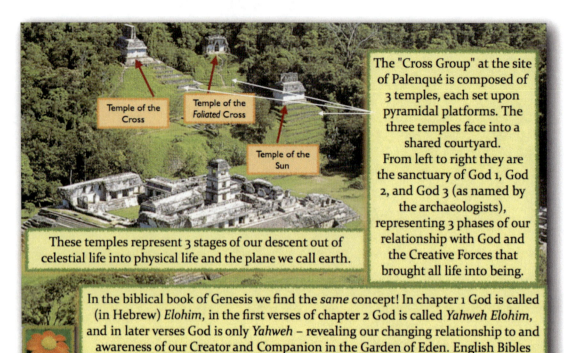

The "Cross Group" at the site of Palenqué is composed of 3 temples, each set upon pyramidal platforms. The three temples face into a shared courtyard.
From left to right they are the sanctuary of God 1, God 2, and God 3 (as named by the archaeologists), representing 3 phases of our relationship with God and the Creative Forces that brought all life into being.

These temples represent 3 stages of our descent out of celestial life into physical life and the plane we call earth.

In the biblical book of Genesis we find the *same* concept! In chapter 1 God is called (in Hebrew) *Elohim*, in the first verses of chapter 2 God is called *Yahweh Elohim*, and in later verses God is only *Yahweh* – revealing our changing relationship to and awareness of our Creator and Companion in the Garden of Eden. English Bibles translate these names as *God*, *Lord God*, and then just *Lord*.

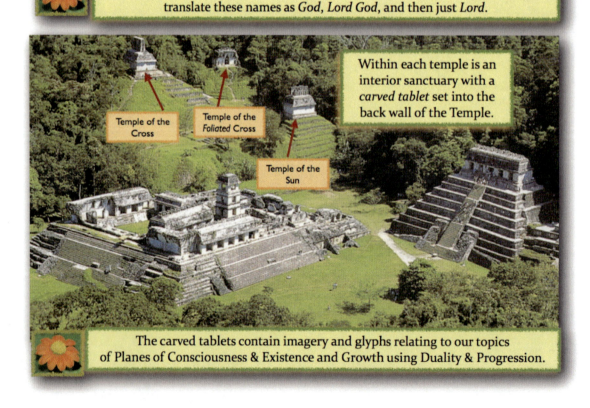

Within each temple is an interior sanctuary with a *carved tablet* set into the back wall of the Temple.

The carved tablets contain imagery and glyphs relating to our topics of Planes of Consciousness & Existence and Growth using Duality & Progression.

This is called the Temple of the Cross because of the cross-like image on its main tablet, symbolizing the world tree. This image presents the Maya's awareness of the nearly universal idea of the *axis mundi*. This temple was also known as the North House (*xaman yotoot*) and in this way is identified with the cosmic hearthstone, which the Paddler Gods planted at the place where light and warmth first occurred. It was from this northern hearthstone that the Maize God sprouted.

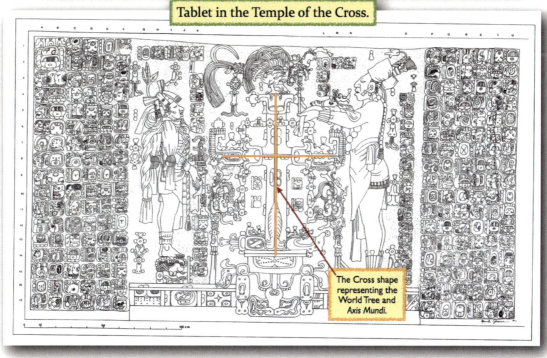

Tablet in the Temple of the Cross.

The Cross shape representing the World Tree and Axis Mundi.

Tablet in the Temple of the Cross.

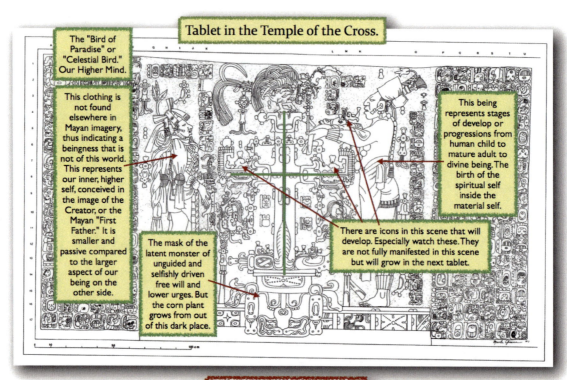

The "Bird of Paradise" or "Celestial Bird." Our Higher Mind.

This clothing is not found elsewhere in Mayan imagery, thus indicating a beingness that is not of this world. This represents our inner, higher self, conceived in the image of the Creator, or the Mayan "First Father." It is smaller and passive compared to the larger aspect of our being on the other side.

The mask of the latent monster of unguided and selfishly driven free will and lower urges. But the corn plant grows from out of this dark place.

This being represents stages of develop or progressions from human child to mature adult to divine being. The birth of the spiritual self inside the material self.

There are icons in this scene that will develop. Especially watch these. They are not fully manifested in this scene but will grow in the next tablet.

The "World Tree"

The concept of a "World Tree" is ancient & multicultural. Its branches reach to the sky and higher realms of consciousness, and its roots reach into the underworld and subconscious realms, and its trunk is the realm of awareness that we are most familiar with.

This is an Aztec version.

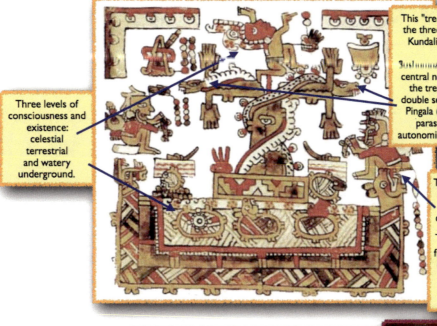

Three levels of consciousness and existence: celestial terrestrial and watery underground.

This "tree" also represents the three pathways of the Kundalini from the Yoga Sutras: Sushumna (cerebrospinal or central nervous system) as the tree trunk, and the double serpents of Ida and Pingala (sympathetic and parasympathetic, or autonomic nervous system).

The life force in the unconscious or subliminal realms can bite you in the ___, but of course you and I learn from these events - right? Well, maybe it takes a few of them before we really learn.

This odd little plate reveals a hole in the World Tree through which "humans" are entering this plane of existence and the many strange forces influencing this realm!

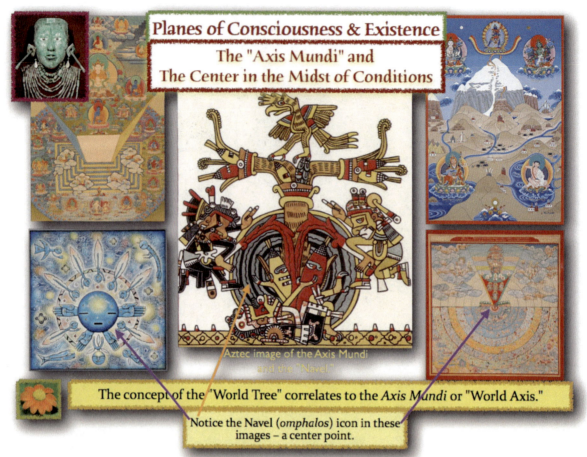

Aztec image of the Axis Mundi and the "Navel."

The concept of the "World Tree" correlates to the *Axis Mundi* or "World Axis."

Notice the Navel (*omphalos*) icon in these images – a center point.

Macrocosm (universal reality)

The Axis Mundi (world axis), in religion or mythology, is the *celestial* pole and *earth* pole, revealing a connection between sky and earth where the four compass directions meet, and the higher and lower planes, including the underworld. Along this axis travel and communication may be made between the higher and lower realms. Communication from lower realms may ascend to higher ones, blessings and guidance from higher realms may descend to lower ones. Along the Axis Mundi is the Navel (*omphalos*), where it all began and like an umbilical cord, it provides nourishment to all. The axis mundi symbol is found in most cultures that have mystical practices and belief systems. The Axis Mundi is often represented in mandalas.

Microcosm (self's individual reality)

The place one occupies is where he/she stands at the center of the world. This space serves as a microcosm of order because it is known and settled – although, the person may be seeking more understanding. Outside the boundaries of the self are foreign realms. They are unfamiliar or not ordered, and are thus represented in myths and imagery as chaos, death, darkness, monstrous, and night time. From the center one may venture in any of the four cardinal directions, making discoveries, and establishing new centers as new realms become known and settled. In this way the immature psyche grows, becoming more aware of the many dimensions of life – both within itself and throughout the cosmos. Eventually, the inner and outer become one.

In the microcosm of our personal inner world the axis and "navel" are states of consciousness and vibrations that bring us renewal and centeredness, a centeredness that fills us with peace and a clearer sense of self and self's ideals. Meditation and reflection help us to realize this.

In *macrocosm* of our whole being and the cosmos, the axis and "navel" connect us to the portals and pathways to a much bigger reality than this limited physical-material life being lived mostly in our 3-D personality – missing our soul life and its relationship to the Creator and Creative Forces of Infinity.

The entire front wall and mansard roof of the Temple of the Foliated Cross have fallen, which gives the building its unusual appearance. In the Maya Cosmological Order, the *Foliated* Cross represents the locations of the heavens, earth, and the underworld, and how they are connected to the plane we live on most of the time! The Foliated Cross is much more elaborate then the Cross, as adult life is more complicated than childhood life.

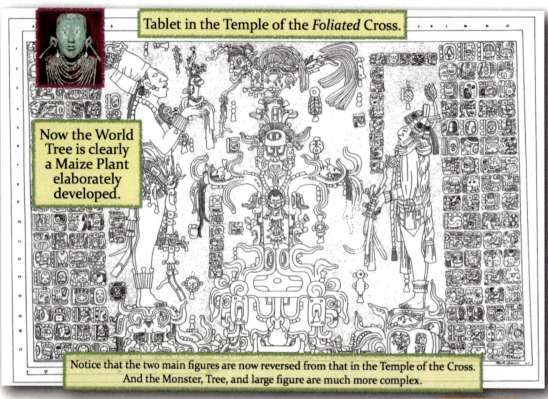

Tablet in the Temple of the *Foliated* Cross.

Now the World Tree is clearly a Maize Plant elaborately developed.

Notice that the two main figures are now reversed from that in the Temple of the Cross. And the Monster, Tree, and large figure are much more complex.

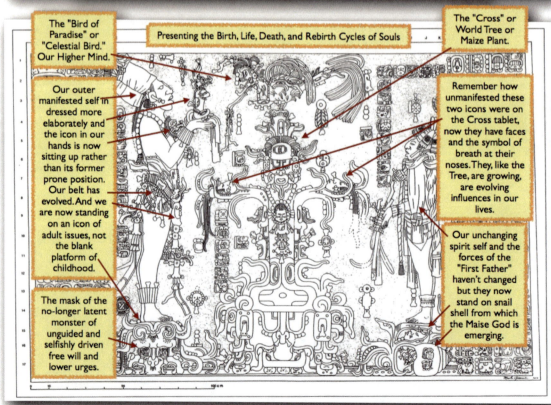

Presenting the Birth, Life, Death, and Rebirth Cycles of Souls

The "Bird of Paradise" or "Celestial Bird." Our Higher Mind.

Our outer manifested self in dressed more elaborately and the icon in our hands is now sitting up rather than its former prone position. Our belt has evolved. And we are now standing on an icon of adult issues, not the blank platform of childhood.

The mask of the no-longer latent monster of unguided and selfishly driven free will and lower urges.

The "Cross" or World Tree or Maize Plant.

Remember how unmanifested these two icons were on the Cross tablet, now they have faces and the symbol of breath at their noses. They, like the Tree, are growing, are evolving influences in our lives.

Our unchanging spirit self and the forces of the "First Father" haven't changed but they now stand on snail shell from which the Maise God is emerging.

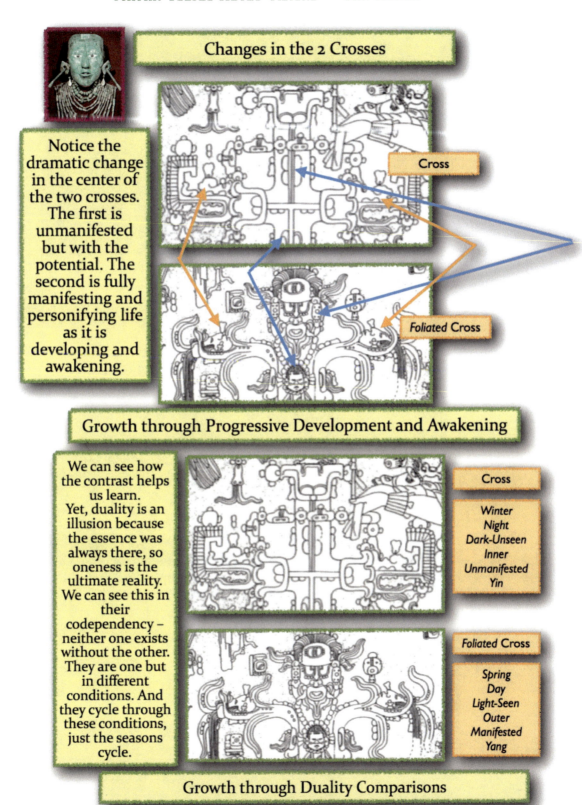

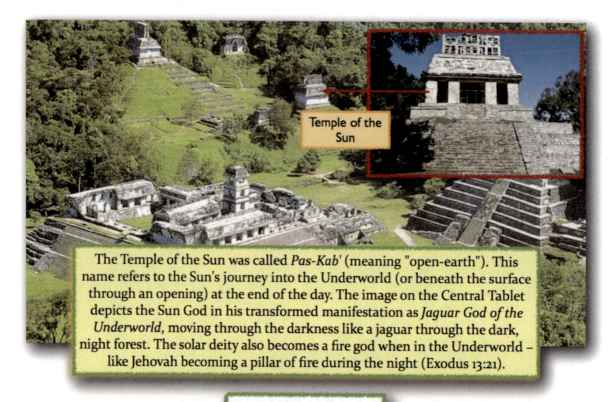

Temple of the Sun

The Temple of the Sun was called *Pas-Kab'* (meaning "open-earth"). This name refers to the Sun's journey into the Underworld (or beneath the surface through an opening) at the end of the day. The image on the Central Tablet depicts the Sun God in his transformed manifestation as *Jaguar God of the Underworld*, moving through the darkness like a jaguar through the dark, night forest. The solar deity also becomes a fire god when in the Underworld – like Jehovah becoming a pillar of fire during the night (Exodus 13:21).

Temple of the Sun

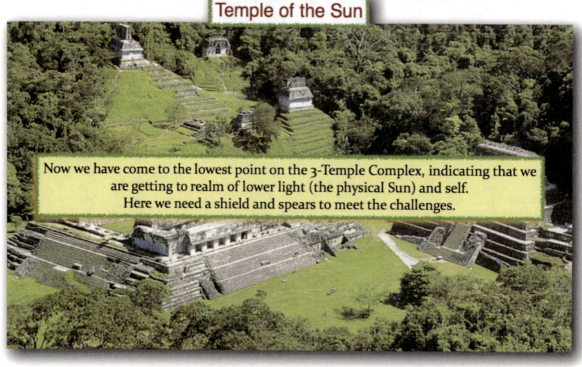

Now we have come to the lowest point on the 3-Temple Complex, indicating that we are getting to realm of lower light (the physical Sun) and self.
Here we need a shield and spears to meet the challenges.

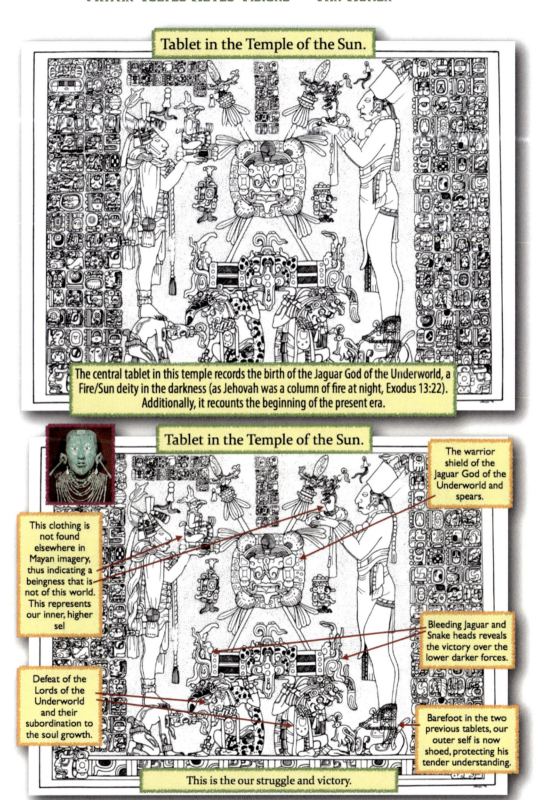

Tablet in the Temple of the Sun.

The central tablet in this temple records the birth of the Jaguar God of the Underworld, a Fire/Sun deity in the darkness (as Jehovah was a column of fire at night, Exodus 13:22). Additionally, it recounts the beginning of the present era.

Tablet in the Temple of the Sun.

The warrior shield of the Jaguar God of the Underworld and spears.

This clothing is not found elsewhere in Mayan imagery, thus indicating a beingness that is not of this world. This represents our inner, higher sel

Bleeding Jaguar and Snake heads reveals the victory over the lower darker forces.

Defeat of the Lords of the Underworld and their subordination to the soul growth.

Barefoot in the two previous tablets, our outer self is now shoed, protecting his tender understanding.

This is the our struggle and victory.

Treasures of Wisdom Inside Temples and Chambers

Temple 3: Water & Fire!

Teotihuacán Complex

Some of the most revealing content about Mesoamerican concepts of soul life are found on the walls of temples and chambers. We now enter a complex that was called:

"The Place Where Gods were Born"

Teotihuacán Temple/Pyramid Complex

There are many temples and two major pyramids on this amazing site. The famous Sun and Moon pyramids are dynamic features, as are the many flat-top temples along the pathway called, "The Avenue of the Dead," but this is the avenue of the *Living Dead*, or souls. Again we find a court yard with a central altar (more on altars later). Our focus, however, is further down the Avenue to the Quetzalcoatl Temple beyond the massive Sun Pyramid.

Pyramid of the Sun is that way.

The A.R.E. tour group entering the Quetzalcoatl Temple Complex

(above) We have walked down the Avenue of the Dead to the Quetzalcoatl Temple(s) and are going to find the opening that allows us to enter in between the two pyramidal temples - or one temple with a large opening between its two parts.

(left) Here you see our group moving in between the two pyramidal temples to an inner section with the major symbolic teachings that we need for our studies. If you look closely you can see some of the symbols on the side of the temple wall. On the next page you see those symbols and their meaning.

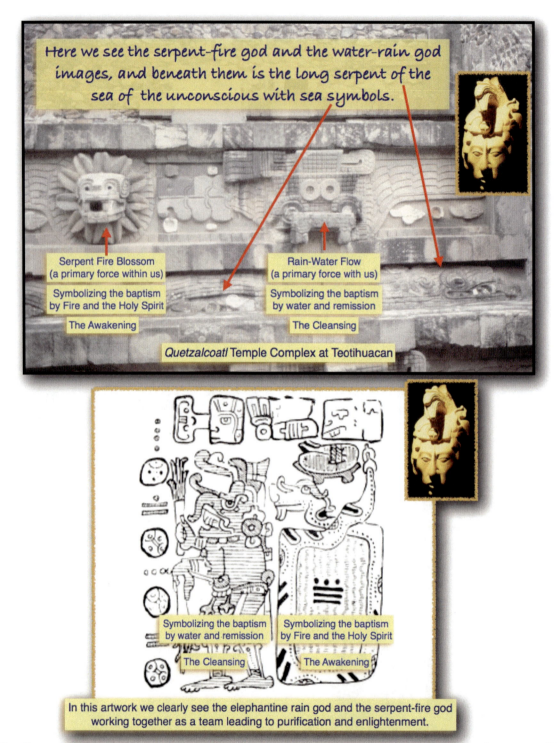

The "revealed" or exoteric teachings of the Bible are likened to water, as in the verse: "O all who thirst, come for water." (Isaiah 55:1) And the "hidden" or esoteric teachings of the Bible are likened to fire, as in this verse: "For are My words not like fire?" (Jeremiah 23:29).

And we find this statement: "Do not fear, for the Lord your God is a consuming fire." (Deuteronomy 9:3 and Hebrews 12:29) John the Baptist explained: "I baptize you with water for the remission of sin; but he who is mightier than I is coming, the thong of whose sandals I am not worthy to untie; he will baptize you with the Holy Spirit and with fire." (Matthew 3:11, Mark 1:8, Luke 3:16, John 1:26)

We have already seen how the shedding of Bloodletting was a way of cleansing ("no remission of sin without shedding of blood"), but Water and Fire are two more stages of every entity's soul growth: 1. *ablution*, from Latin *abluere*, meaning "to wash away" – ritually cleansing one of sin and weakness using water; and, 2. *inflame*, so as to arouse one to a higher, ecstatic level of being by the consuming fire of Spirit that burns off the lower nature and urges – as in "burn up the chaff with unquenchable fire." (Matthew 3:12) On this wall we see the two stages depicted by a water being and a serpent-dragon (see images on previous page and below). The image below is suggestive of the *Yoga Sutra* concept of *chakra and lotus*, with the serpent-dragon coming out of a flower – chakra is *fiery-wheel energy* and lotus is *illuminating consciousness*.

These – blood sacrifice, washing away errors, and fire burning off dross – are *metaphors* for crucifying selfish gratifications for the higher purpose of gaining soulful contentment through harmony with Forces of Life and Nature. One does not need to cut the body, bathe in holy water or be consumed by fire – only one's heart and mind needs these *inner*, transformative influences to rise to their true soul self.

Here's close-up of the serpent-dragon head emerging from flower of life. This symbolizes the rise of the serpentine kundalini through the lotus blossom, or the combination of vibrations-energy and awareness-mind.

Treasures of Wisdom Inside Temples and Chambers
Temple 4: Uxmal - The Magician Within Us

MAGIC was an integral part of ancient Mesoamerican life. They believed that life was conceived through magic, Nature displays magic in her ways, and the people saw magic happen in their lives and the lives of those around them. Of course certain people displayed an easy skill with magic and magical ways, these became the so-called "shamans." The word "*shaman*" originated from the Tungusic Evenki language of North Asia. The term was first applied by western anthropologists who were outside observers of the ancient religion of the Turks and Mongols, as well as those of the neighboring Tungusic- and Samoyedic-speaking peoples. When the Russians started conquering and colonizing Siberia, they came upon shamans among the Evenk people. A shaman has access to the unseen world of spirit, and is able evoke the spirit(s). Typically such people entered a trance state during a ritual, practicing divination and healing. The term is now applied to the magicians of Mesoamerica. Important to our study is that WE ALL possess latent magical skill – *there is a Magician within each of us.*

Uxmal (oosh-mal) and the Magician's Pyramid

Pyramid of the Magician — Higher Consciousness Training — The Magician Within Us

In this sculpture the artist is depicting three layers of our being and consciousness. The little human face is our daily personality self, the face with the stripes is our deeper soul and subconscious self, and the larger, less individualized, less personal face (the bigger part of us) is our infinite, eternal self and superconscious mind.

And though they look separate and often act separately, they are layered in the wholeness of our being – whether we are conscious of this or not.

It is not by the human self taking thought that we bring the influence of the higher mind and magic, and God's powers into our lives. Rather, it is by the human self *subduing* its dominance and seeking the original, greater self, the immortal self that the magic of renewal and illumination occurs. When done properly, our awareness expands and magic is a natural result.

Conjuring or Evoking the Unseen Forces

I realize how scary this may appear to some of us but if we go through it carefully, and always hold to Edgar Cayce's guidance to *cooperate* and *coordinate* with the Divine Forces, with God, then we can learn to awaken the Magician Within Us SAFELY, learning to bring the unseen forces into the seen.

It was widely thought that Mesoamerican conjuring and vision-quests were induced by bloodletting. Researchers are now casting some doubt on this. Also, hallucinogenics were not always used. Conjuring may have been done with or without the aid of psychoactive substances. For example, in *Maya Cosmos*, Parker has made a case for trance dancing – like Sufi dancing, the Whirling Dervishes – as a means of accessing the supernatural. We see some evidence of this in our study, as in the illustration of "trance dancing" in the codices on the next page.

Edgar Cayce taught the following:

"In that as is called mysticism or magic, may the entity excel – will these be tempered by those of the forces of love, duty, and reason." (1714-1)

"In the understanding of magic or mysterious forces – whether as to song, music, or of precious stones, and even these that have to do with the odors – may the entity gain, conquer self, and develop through these experiences; so long as the DESIRE is in accord with that universal force or development called, God." (1714-1)

There are "abilities of individuals to use the unseen forces; or to work in what would be called by some MAGIC, by others those influences in which the elementals were used for activities upon the higher tension of the mental forces of individuals. (1724-4)

"The entity was among those who by its own wits made what would be called now sorceries or divinations, using charm and magic as a means to attain those desires and purposes. Hence in the present all things pertaining to charm, sacred formulas, societies, initiations, the ritual of varied groups are of interest to the entity, no matter whether these are in the darkest minds of men or in the higher ritualistic orders.

"These abilities were not used for other than material things. Thus, while they have the material hold, they must be watched and guarded against becoming the thing you worship, rather than the spiritual. Hence the warning that has been indicated to the entity. It is the spirit with which you do a thing, the purpose that brings weal or woe in its effect in the experience." (3285-2)

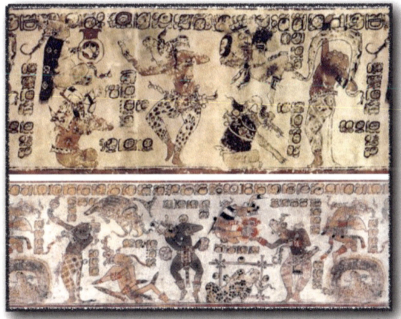

Codices showing Trance Dancing, likely with the help of psychoactive potions and smokes.

The ancient Maya had ready access to a number of psychoactive substances, but they did not always use these for conjuring. In the Cayce readings there is mention of "potions" being used by the Ancient Egyptian priests and priestesses to generate certain conditions – so it's likely from Cayce's view that the Mesoamericans did the same in some instances, but not all.

Trance dancing is common among Native Americans in North American as well as Mesoamericans – likely with the help of psychoactive potions and smokes.

Way'ob means "sleeping," but with the connotation of magical, mystical sleep. One who can enter this state of being is a Nah'ual (or Nagual, both pronounced na'wal). A Nah'ual is also a human being who has the power to magically turn him- or herself into an animal form. Such a Nah'ual is believed to use his powers for good or evil according to his/her personality. Mesoamericans believed in *therianthropy*, wherein humans have an animal counterpart to which their life force is linked, and the animal counterpart has both the strengths and weaknesses of that animal. In English the word *Nagual* comes from Mesoamerican myths about human beings who has the power to magically turn themselves into animal forms – most commonly donkeys, turkeys, and dogs but can also transform into more powerful jaguars and pumas. Nagual is often defined as a transforming witch or wizard. In Yucatec ethnography, the transformation may also be a ghost or apparition – and these latter two are of interest to us today because we leave our physical, human nature asleep on the bed, releasing our ghost to enter the other realms of existence and activity.

It helps our modern minds to think of conjuring as evoking the "Spirit of God" to draw us into a higher state of consciousness and existence in order for us to participate as co-creators with our Creator – improving our health and lives. By this means our spiritual powers emerge and we have better protection, behavior, and assistance.

Before we begin, Cayce would have guided us to determine in whom we believe and what is our ideal purpose for regaining our godly powers. He would have asked us: "Are these for self? self-gratification? self-exaltation? Or are they for the greater good – as God sees such?" Co-creators implies *cooperation* between us and our Creator and Nature – and Cayce often gave an affirmation or mantra: "Not my will but Thy Will be done in and through me for the greater good of all concerned."

We are NOT conjuring "familiar spirits" or discarnate guides or entities – ONLY the Infinite, Holy, Creator of our being and all life – nothing lower. Of course, if the Creator sends a spirit guide, then that's fine.

Let's begin by studying some key Mayan imagery and instructions. This imagery has to do with the powerful – and occasionally overwhelming – LIFE FORCES, within and around us.

We begin with a conjuring scene on Vessels K1198 and K0719. The originals are difficult to see due to aging, so we'll use modern reproductions of the images so we can see clearly. Though the image is strange, it is translatable and conveys metaphysical meaning to help us understand the Mesoamerican concept of conjuring.

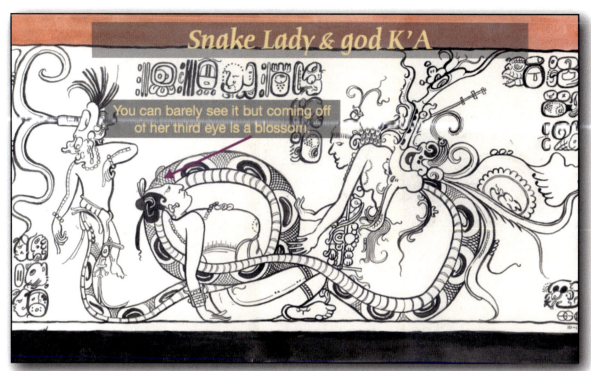

Snake Lady has 3 layers to her, she is human, semi-divine, and divine. In this scene she has conjured the lightning god K'A (from *k'awiil*, meaning "powerful one," and often referred to simply as "god K"). God K has her entwined in his serpentine powers, again using the kundalini concept of the Life Force energy. It helps if we consider these two as parts of our whole being, not separate entities. K is in two forms, one at the serpent's tail (left) and one at the maw (mouth) of the serpent (right). In the oldest Mayan imagery, god K has one leg that is a serpent, revealing his association with the Life Force, as lightning would be. A smokey expression is coming out of his forehead, indicating mystical connections – especially to the primordial times, the times of the *origin* of the Life Forces. Shifting from the great serpent's tail to his maw (mouth) we again see god K emerging and directly getting involved with Snake Lady in an intimate manner. The Life Forces are also the sexual forces as well as other forces within us. And though there is some sensuality in this image, its more about the Life Forces than sexual activity. God K's smokey symbol now emerges from the topknot on his head, his crown chakra, rather than his third eye when at the tail of the serpent. These two chakras (crown and third eye) are key to awakening the Life Forces within us. This great serpent is known as *Och Chan*, and is the "visioning serpent" for communing with realms and planes beyond the physical world and personal human reality. The conjuring of god K has brought the powers of the *visioning serpent* into the Lady's realm of existence and she may now commune with the higher realms. Such communing was often directed toward ancestors as well as gods for the purpose of getting guidance and information. It was considered to be a supernatural experience, transcending the human, time-space existence. Notice the expression on the face of Snake Lady, her mind is obviously elsewhere and she is seeing with her mind's eye not her physical eyes. On her third eye is a blossom, indicating *blooming* awareness.

In this next closeup we see qualities of god K that reveal the oneness of our condition in the higher realms of life. Notice that the Lightning god has both a symbolic vagina (top arrow) and penis (middle arrow), the yin & yang again. From these genitals extends a blossom (bottom arrow) with pistil (female) and stamen (male). You might think they should call the male part the pistil, but in flowers the female has the *pistol*. (just a little joke on my part - forgive me)

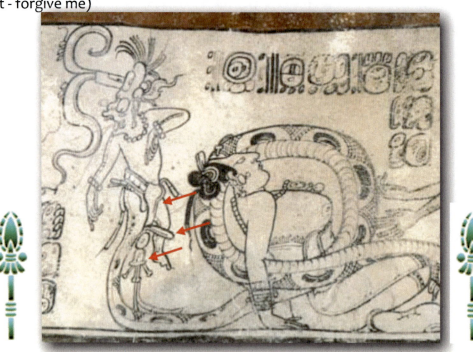

The androgyny of the original being created in Genesis 1 was not separated into separate gender-specific bodies until Genesis 2:21-22. God K retains the original androgyny of the united soul in higher dimensions of existence. This image of a man emerging from the body of a raised serpent is the classic representation of conjuring the higher forces, the Life Forces into greater presence. Notice that it is rising out of the bowl of blood drops on sacred offering paper – indicating that the outer self must sacrifice its dominate presence in order for the powers of the inner self to emerge.

In this illustration (right) we see a Mayan who has successfully conjured the unseen forces and entered into the higher realms. He is comfortable stepping above the now submissive serpent energy during the process of rising to higher levels of perception to gain insight and guidance. His facial expression and physical demeanor reveal that he has the right motivation, state of mind, and attitude. And though there are many distracting influences, he is focused on his mission.

The Womb of Emergence

Chicomoztoc, "the place of the seven caves," from Historia Tolteca-Chichimeca

The tiny seed knew that in order to grow, it needed to be dropped in dirt, covered in darkness, and struggle to reach the Light...

"Truly I say to you, unless a grain of wheat falls into the earth and dies, it remains alone; but if it dies, it bears much fruit. He who loves his life loses it, and he who hates his life in this world will keep it for eternal life." (John 12:24-25)

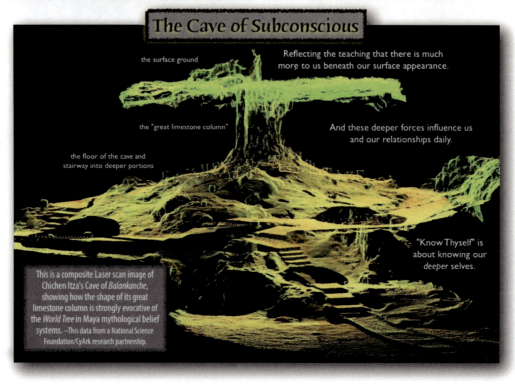

The Cave of Subconscious

the surface ground

Reflecting the teaching that there is much more to us beneath our surface appearance.

the "great limestone column"

And these deeper forces influence us and our relationships daily.

the floor of the cave and stairway into deeper portions

"Know Thyself" is about knowing our *deeper selves*.

This is a composite Laser scan image of Chichen Itza's Cave of *Balankanche*, showing how the shape of its great limestone column is strongly evocative of the *World Tree* in Maya mythological belief systems. —This data from a National Science Foundation/CyArk research partnership.

The 7 Caves and 5 Races

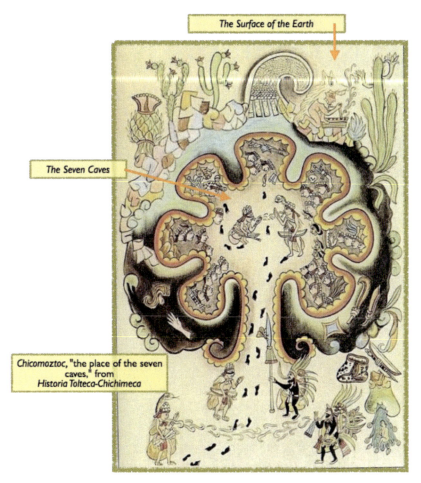

Chicomoztoc, "the place of the seven caves," from *Historia Tolteca-Chichimeca*

The first tribes of the maize-people journey to the place of the Seven Caves and Seven Canyons (*Tulan Zuiva*) to "powwow" about their feelings of being lost in matter and earthiness. There they received their patron gods, including *Tohil*, a patron god of the Quiché and the source of fire, the element of that age. When the people finally conclude their conference and leave the Seven Canyons, they no longer speak one language and now travel in five different groups, five directions, and exactly as Cayce read the Akasha about the original five races. They separate and go to five specific locations on the planet Earth. Here is Cayce's explanation of this strange occurrence.

Edgar Cayce and the 5 Races – 5 Locations – 5 Senses (364-13):

- **YELLOW** —Mu/Lemuria-Gobi —Hearing
- **BROWN** —Mu/Lemuria-Andes —Smell/Scent
- **RED** —Atlantis — Touch/Feel
- **BLACK** —Nubia —Taste
- **WHITE** —Caucasus Mountains —Sight

The original idea was that the one body of souls, the so-called "Morning Stars" that sang together as they descended from heaven (as the "Children of God") would divide into 5 groups, each mastering one of the seven senses (a division of labor), then return as one benefited by what each group had gained.

"Mom" – Coatlicue, meaning "Snakes-her-skirt"
(pronounced *koh-at-lee-kway*)

This massive basalt statue, over 10' high (3.5 meters), is located in the National Museum of Anthropology and History in Mexico City.

The legend and lore concerning Coatlicue is fantastically metaphorical and retells a similar story found in many ancient cultures around the world. She was a princess who kept the temple on Sacred Mountain (*Coatepec*, "Snake Mountain"). One day while doing her duties feathers fell from Heaven and lodged in her belt. These feathers (reminiscent of the god Quetzalcoatl, immaculately impregnated the princess (note: she was not a virgin, as so many other immaculately impregnated young women were in these classic stories). Growing in her womb was the patron god of the Aztecs, *Huitzilopochtli* (pronounced, *who-it-zi-lo-poke-li*). His name means the *Hummingbird of the South* or *Blue Hummingbird*. He was the supreme god of the gods. He was god of the sun, war, gold, and the Aztec capital city *Tenochtitlán*. His *Nagual* animal spirit was none other than the famous Aztec eagle.

Why would the mother of the major Aztec god be depicted a terrifying serpent and skull in her belly region? Again, the Mesoamericans were much more into the Shadow than the ancient Egyptians. The Shadow, as taught by Swiss psychologist Carl Jung, exists as part of the *unconscious* mind and is composed of *repressed* urges, forces, weaknesses, desires, and basic instincts of human nature. These are what the Mesoamericans saw as "the Dark Forces" of the Underworld. This Jungian archetype is often described as the darker side of our psyche, representing wildness, chaos, and the unknown. Jung believed that these latent dispositions are present in all of us! And though some people may deny this element of their own psyche, it is growing within them. This denial often leads to projecting their dark side onto others. Jung suggested that the shadow can appear in dreams or visions and may take a variety of forms. He even said the Shadow could appear as a snake, a monster, a demon, a dragon or some other dark, wild or exotic figure – like Coatlicue! Yet, despite how terrifying and fearsome she appears, she is not an enemy, rather, she is the channel through which our greater good, our better self can be born – our own hero Hummingbird *Huitzilopochtli!*

Ancient Altars

The Famous Jaguar Altar Located at La Venta
Below is a closeup on the stylized Jaguar

Below is a line drawing of the altar's front

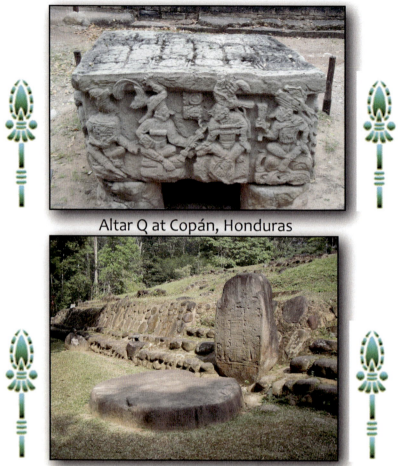

Altar Q at Copán, Honduras

Circular altar and Calendar Stele at Tak'alik Ab'aj, Guatemala
3,000 years ago, around 1000 BC

This circular altar was believed to be used for human sacrifice, but Edgar Cayce's readings of the Akasha stated that they were initially used for cleansing the body. The "channels" were not initially for blood but for removing excess water and oils.

Circular Altar at Caracol, Belize – appears to be usable for cleansing the body rather than killing it.

Circular Altar at Piedras Negras, Guatemala

Edgar Cayce on Altars

"The altars upon which there were the cleansings of the bodies of individuals (not human sacrifice; for this came much later with the injection of the Mosaic [Moses people], and those activities of that area), these were later the altars upon which individual activities - that would today be termed hate, malice, selfishness, self-indulgence - were cleansed from the body through the ceremony, through the rise of initiates from the sources of light, that came from the stones upon which the angels of light during the periods gave their expression to the peoples." (EC 5750-1)

"The stones that are circular, that were of the magnetized influence upon which the Spirit of the One spoke to those peoples as they gathered in their service, are of the earliest Atlantean activities in religious service." (EC 5750-1)

"The pyramid, the altars before the doors of the varied temple activities, was an injection from the people of Oz and Mu; and will be found to be separate portions, and that referred to in the Scripture as high places of family altars, family gods, that in many portions of the world became again the injection into the activities of groups in various portions, as gradually there were the turnings of the people to the satisfying and gratifying of self's desires, or as the Baal or Baalilal activities again entered the peoples respecting their associations with those truths of light that came from the gods to the peoples, to mankind, in the earth." (EC 5750-1)

Cayce's reference to Baal as a dark force is found in the writings of the 1600s concerning the 7 Princes of Hell, with Baal being the leader of the dark forces. Baal was also the counter cult to the Hebrew Yahweh (I Kings 18). For Cayce, self and selfishness were the dark forces, and they could be so subtle in their possession of well-intended seekers who didn't have their ideals firmly established before raising the powers.

Altars for Rebirthing the Spirit-Soul

There are also altars that appear to be depicting "emergence" or rebirth.

Altar at La Venta

That Cayce teaching that we read (EC 5750-1) is fascinating: "the altars upon which individual activities – that would today be termed hate, malice, selfishness, self-indulgence – were cleansed from the body through the ceremony, through the rise of initiates from the sources of light, that came from the stones upon which the angels of light during the periods gave their expression to the peoples." Angels of light working through special stones on these altars reveals the presence of beings beyond incarnates. Cayce explained that these stones were *magnetic* and affected the body and mind of participants in the ceremonies.

Edgar Cayce on Magnetic Stones at Altars

Cayce taught that in Atlantis crystals were used to commune with the "Spirit of the One," who "spoke" *through* the crystals to the people. This could in the manner that an old crystal radio operated, extracting a signal and converting it to sound.

Magnetite

After the discovery of the formation of the mineral magnetite in certain animals, scientists began to study *biomagnetism*. Magnetite was found in the brain linings of bees, termites, rhinoceros, even in some bacteria, and most importantly in *carrier pigeons*. This magnetite is in the form of very tiny crystals in the living organisms. Then it was found *in the brains of humans*, and the field of study became serious, trying to understand why. Prior to this magnetite was believed to only have formed as a result of the geological processes related to volcanoes. In pigeons and bees it appeared that the magnetite helped with navigation, but why in humans? In 1990 it was found in the cerebral cortex, cerebellum, and in the lining surrounding the brain and spinal cord. Studies of these magnetic crystals have revealed that they are in fact *manufactured by the living cells*, and arranged in such a way that the maximum magnetic effect is achieved. Some scientists are speculating that magnetic brain tissues in animals provide animals with some of their psychic abilities. For example, it is common for animals to behave abnormally just before a major earthquake or disaster. Could the magnetite in their brains be responsible for the perception of subtle changes in the earths geomagnetic field? Wearing magnetic jewelry or placing magnets on the body has become a popular practice. Magnetite is a type of rock that has strong magnetic properties. When it comes in close contact with the body, it realigns the vital "chi" energy, removing energy blockages that cause pain due to imbalances in the energy flow. Many people are now wearing bracelets and necklaces made from magnetite stones. In some cases it is because it has been found to relieve pain.

Hematite

Hematite gets its name from the Greek *haimo* for "blood," because of the color of its powder. This stone is a compact form of iron oxide. Natural hematite is rare and expensive. These beads are made from hematite pieces and dust that have been ground up and fused into shape. Some companies call them "hemalike", "hemalyke", or "hematine" to designate they are *manufactured*. A wide variety of health benefits have been attributed to magnetic jewelry. It is said to maintain the *natural charge of the nerve cells*, thus reducing pain; increase the healing process; boost the immune system; improve quality of sleep; relieve ailments of the hands, wrists, and fingers; and generally enhance physical energy and vitality. It also is reported to help tension headaches and light migraines. In some circumstances people have recorded a difference within 48 hours of putting on the stones. The story behind *natural* hematite is still relevant to this gemstone, especially considering real hematite is used to make it. Magnetic jewelry can cause the iron in the blood to act as a conductor of the magnetic field, thus producing magnetic energy. This purportedly improves blood flow which in turn increases the efficiency of oxygen & nutrient delivery to the tissues.

UNSEEN ASPECTS OF LIFE

(right) This is a *completed* sculpture! Yes, it was intended to look like this – notice the painted portion of this statue. What artist would begin painting before he or she had finished the sculpting? So what is the artist attempting to show us? The artist is showing the un-manifested and the manifested, the unformed and the formed, the unseen and the seen. It is transformation from one condition to another. This is a concept that we need to grasp if we are to tap into the source of magic. As Cayce taught: "The Unseen forces are more powerful than the seen," and we have to get in touch with those unseen, un-manifested, hidden forces.

"As is conceded, even by the most pessimistic, UNSEEN forces are the more powerful than those seen – or realities. The dreamer, the visionary, those who attune themselves to the infinite, the more often they receive the more infinite power, for those attunements will bring into being those as of the realities of the UNSEEN forces being as COORDINANT in their activity, as the night follows the day, the moon sheds its light from the activity of the giver of light, the sun." (EC 262-8)

"There is no difference in the unseen world to that that is visible, save in the unseen so much greater expanse or space may be covered! It's a NATURAL experience! It's NOT an unnatural! Don't seek for unnatural or supernatural! It is the natural – it is Nature – it is God's activity! His associations with man. His DESIRE to make for man a way for an understanding! Is there seen or understood fully that illustration that was given of the Son of man, that while those in the ship were afraid because of the elements, the Master of the sea and of the elements slept? What associations may there have been with that sleep? Was it a natural withdrawing? yet when spoken to, the sea and the winds obeyed His voice. You may do even as He, will you make yourself aware – whether that awareness through the ability of those forces within self to communicate with, understand, those elements of the spiritual life IN the conscious and unconscious, these be one!" (5754-3)

The 3 Mayan Realms of Life are depicted in the Tree of Life above: 1. Life in the Underworld among the roots and soil, 2. life on the surface with the trunk and rings of the ages and passage of time, and 3. in the heavens among the higher branches and leaves in the sky and sunshine. One can be focused in only one of these realms or perhaps two, but the enlightened ones are aware of all 3 realms and their interconnectedness. Curiously, Cayce's visions imply that life and consciousness actually began in the heavens (the branches and leaves, symbolic of the superconscious), then expressed itself in the deep mental realm (the roots and soil, symbolic of the subconscious), and eventually burst forth into the light of the day as an incarnate being (the trunk, the conscious mind, and personality).

The Cycles of TIME
The 7 Ages/Suns of Human Existence

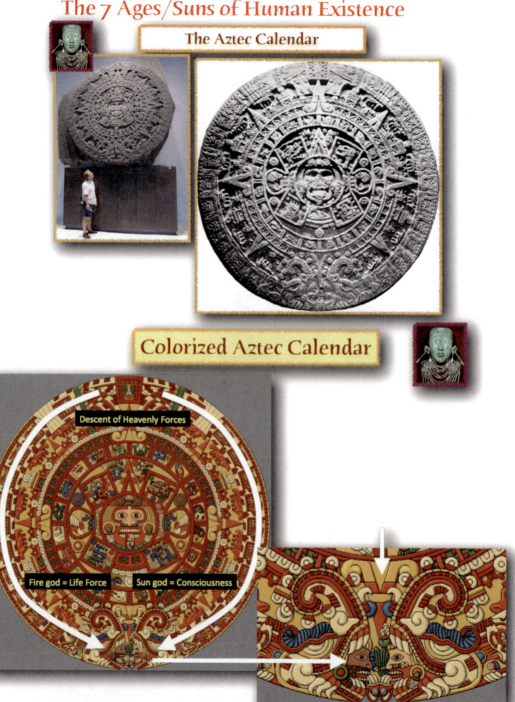

Fire god is the left face emerging from the serpent-dragon, Sun god is the right-side face emerging – each is descending from the higher heavens into matter.

The 7 Ages or "Suns"

In the center of the Eagle Bowl we see stylized depictions of 5 Ages, which the Aztecs called "Suns," as in major Sun cycles. 4 Suns are in squares and the 5th is the circle in the middle with the face of the Sun god in it.

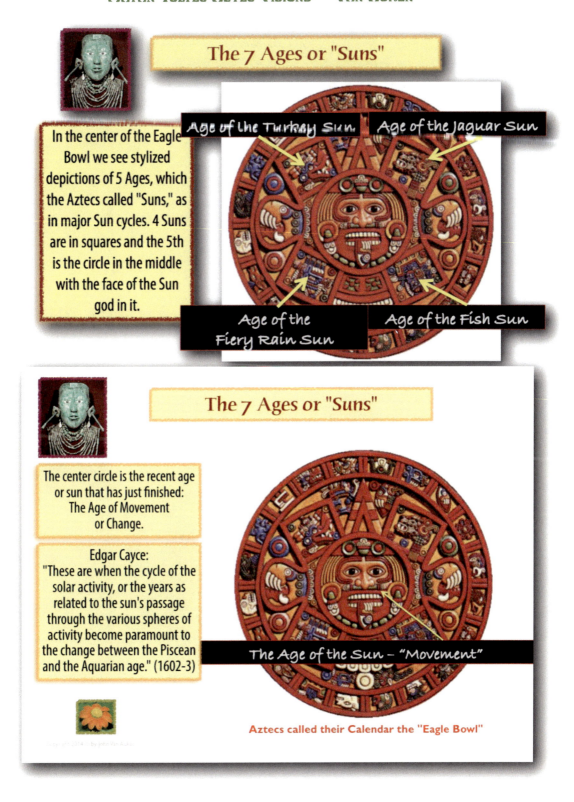

- Age of the Turkey Sun
- Age of the Jaguar Sun
- Age of the Fiery Rain Sun
- Age of the Fish Sun

The 7 Ages or "Suns"

The center circle is the recent age or sun that has just finished: The Age of Movement or Change.

Edgar Cayce:
"These are when the cycle of the solar activity, or the years as related to the sun's passage through the various spheres of activity become paramount to the change between the Piscean and the Aquarian age." (1602-3)

The Age of the Sun – "Movement"

Aztecs called their Calendar the "Eagle Bowl!"

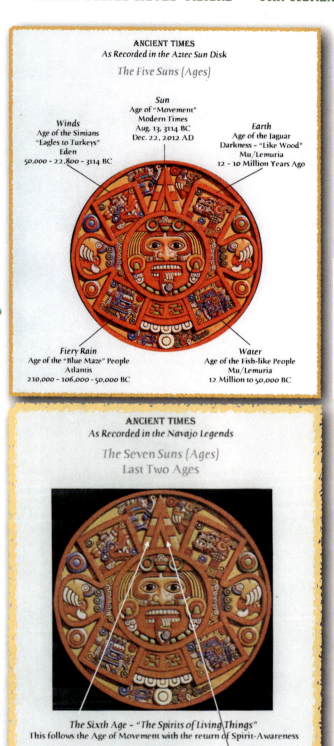

ANCIENT TIMES
As Recorded in the Aztec Sun Disk

The Five Suns (Ages)

Sun
Age of "Movement"
Modern Times
Aug. 13, 3114 BC
Dec. 22, 2012 AD

Winds
Age of the Simians
"Eagles to Turkeys"
Eden
50,000 - 22,800 - 3114 BC

Earth
Age of the Jaguar
Darkness - "Like Wood"
Mu/Lemuria
12 - 10 Million Years Ago

Fiery Rain
Age of the "Blue Maze" People
Atlantis
210,000 - 106,000 - 50,000 BC

Water
Age of the Fish-like People
Mu/Lemuria
12 Million to 50,000 BC

ANCIENT TIMES
As Recorded in the Navajo Legends

The Seven Suns (Ages)
Last Two Ages

The Sixth Age – "The Spirits of Living Things"
This follows the Age of Movement with the return of Spirit-Awareness

The Seventh Age – "The Place of Melting into One"
The Return to original Oneness

An Actual Mayan Calendar Found!

William Saturno of Boston University, who is the archaeologist managing the new discovery published an article in the journal *Science*, he wrote: "The Maya calendar is going to keep going...."

What Saturno found turned out to be a well-perservered mural that includes the oldest known Mayan calendar ever found! This new discovery provides us with clear evidence that the end of this 5,128-year cycle marks *the beginning of a new cycle!* According to Mayan legend, the previous cycle—the one that ended on December 21, 2012—was an era of major change, called the *Age of Movement*. The new finding shows that the calculations include 6,000 years beyond 2012. Anthony Aveni of Colgate University in Hamilton, N.Y., an expert on Mayan astronomy asks, "Why would they go into those numbers if the world is going to come to an end 2012? You could say a number that big at least suggests that time marches on." A new Maya Date reaches to 8000 AD! Interestingly, in the 1500s Nostradamus wrote a letter to his son stating that his visions see far into the future, to the year 3797 AD and beyond.

The Maya-Aztec prophecies see 2 more ages of human experience: The Age of the Spirit of All Living Things followed by the Age of Melting into One (Oneness).

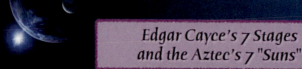

Edgar Cayce's 7 Stages and the Aztec's 7 "Suns"

It's both sequential & cyclical.
We don't just go straight through these stages, we repeat them over and over until we have mastered each stage!

1. World as the Beetle
2. Birth as the Cockerel
3. Mind as the Serpent
4. Wisdom as the Hawk
5. Cross and Crown
6. The Gate, The Door
7. The Way

1. The Jaguar/Darkness
2. The Fish/Horizon
3. Fiery Rain/Blue Maze
4. Simians/Turkeys
5. Movement/Change
6. Spirit of Living Things
7. Return to Oneness

Copyright 2014 © by John Van Auken

The 7 Aspects of the 1

The Only One (*Hunab Ku*) is the infinite, eternal, unborn, undying creator who emanated out of the dreamless sleep of 13 eternities and expressed from his own being the "Heart of Heaven".
The Heart of Heaven sleep in silent contemplation for 7 eternities, eventually emanating from her heart the original 7 gods. The original gods contained the creator of the physical world and all the souls. This creator was one in its essence but is expressed through 7 divinities, as white light through a prism is expressed in the 7 colors of the rainbow: red, orange, yellow, green, blue, indigo, and violet.

Those of you who read my Egyptian Visions book know their feminine creative god was *Iusaaset*, she was the Egyptian "Heart of Heaven" and "Mother of the gods." With Atum she also emanated 7 gods.

A Prism
1
The Light Spectrum: One Ray to Seven

The Seven Gods

The principle motivation of the 7 gods was to create, so they came together and conceived life – firstly, they conceived of the dimension of breath, since breath is life – and eventually they created humans (after 3 tries!).

1. Itzamna (on the throne, founder of the Mayan culture), 2. Tzacol (Sky god of the West, color black), 3. Bitol (Sky god of the East, color red), 4. Tepeu, 5. Gucumatz, 6. Alom (Sky god of the North, color white), and 7. Caholom (Sky god of the South, color yellow). Itzamna, Tepeu, and Gucumatz compose the center of the Cosmos, and the color green.

This is a panoramic view of the "Vase of the Seven Gods."

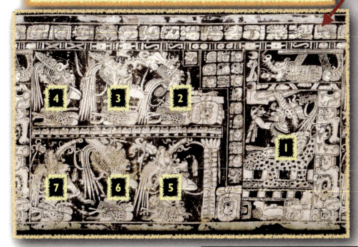

Courtesy of Princeton University

Chakras & Lotuses

Correlate to the:

7 Endocrine Glands
7 Churches of Asia Minor
7 Colors of the Spectrum
7 Notes of the Scale
7 Planets in our System
7 Maidens of Moses
7 Words in the Lord's Prayer

The Secret Body
Arranged for Metaphysical Experiences

Life – Death – Rebirth
In Aztec Lore and Imagery

In this scene we see the Aztec god Xipe Totec (pronounced, *shee-pay tow-tek*) accompanied by the image of god Quetzalcoatl, the Feathered Serpent swallowing a human. In Aztec lore Xipe Totec represents life, death, and rebirth. Quetzalcoatl represents the powerful Kundalini Life Energy of Hinduism. As we learned on page 29, the powerful Forces of Life can give rejuvenation, health, healing, and strength when used properly but they can also cause one to "lose their mind" or be swallowed up by the misuse of the Life Forces. For example, in the late 1900s when Yoga gurus came to the Western cultures they taught kundalini yoga meditation, it was exciting, but a few years later many Westerners were writing books on "kundalini crisis" because they were prepared for the powerful force rising in their bodies and the opening of chakras.

Xipe Totec is known to have "flayed" his body in order to feed humanity, a sacrificial act for the sake of others. In fact, his name means: "Flayed One" in Nahuatl (pronounced *now-wat-tol*), the language of the Aztecs.

In most ancient theologies and initiation training self-sacrifice for a higher good is an integral part of the seeker's path. And, the Mesoamericans carried this idea in their beliefs as well. Xipe Totec gave of himself for the sake of others, that they may be fed and nourished. Giving of oneself to help others is required for full soul growth and enlightenment, it indicates a sense of the oneness to which all are connected, therefore others are part of oneself - this is a major enlightenment. The super powerful Life Energy is mastered by the attitude and discipline found in selflessness for higher purposes. The "serpent" does not sallow the person but instead enhances them, giving them magic (by opening chakras) and wisdom (by opening lotuses).

It is the classic teaching that the right knowledge and practices are ONLY one wing of the Bird of Paradise, the other wing is the RIGHT HEART! And the Bird does not fly with only one wing. One cannot *teach* the right heart – it belongs to the person.

The Dangers of Double Mindedness

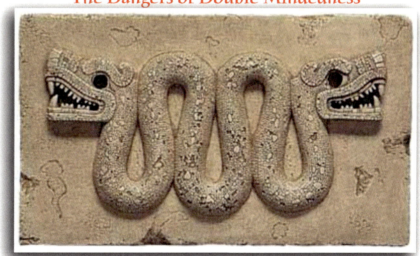

If you look closely at the image on page 96 you will see between Xipe Totec and Quetzalcoatl, and just below the human in Quetzalcoatl's mouth a two-headed snake, and on page 95 you see another image of this. The two-headed snake is a symbol of double-mindedness – attempting to take the Forces of Life, the Kundalini, in two opposing directions, one toward gratification of fleshy desires and another toward higher mental and spiritual vibrations and consciousness. This creates a conflict in the human being. All uses of the Life Forces must be an expression of the true self, which is a spiritual, celestial being temporarily sojourning in an earthly, terrestrial condition. This is not to say that bodily needs and desires cannot be experienced, but they must be an expression of the greater self and not just a gratification of selfish desires. As Jesus once noted, "No one can serve two masters; for either he will hate the one and love the other, or he will be devoted to the one and despise the other. You cannot serve God and mammon." (Matthew 6:24) Again, the physical can be enjoyed but it is to be done as an expression of the spiritual, celestial nature of a soul and not simply as a gratification of the fleshy, earthly, selfish portion of one's being.

Below is a photo of the two-headed serpent in the British Museum.

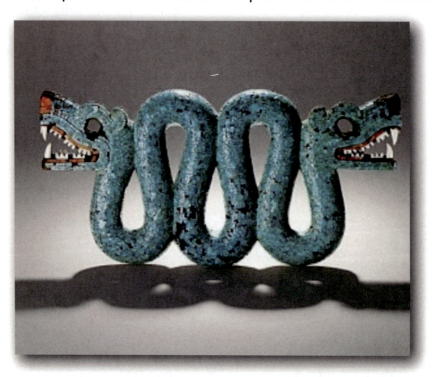

It is composed of pieces of turquoise, spiny oyster shell, and conch shell. The eye holes have residue of beeswax, indicating that they once held objects symbolic of eyes.

Upside-Downess – Two Realities

In the image below to the right we see the two realities:

above and below
inner and outer

The upper face is the higher mind that experiences life from a much different perspective than the lower face. Also, notice the difference in the eyes, indicating that these two levels of consciousness see differently.

Going back to the famous Jaguar altar (below) we see the priest has an upside-down head on top of his natural head, revealing again a consciousness upside-down from our reality, an inner, higher source of awareness and knowing.

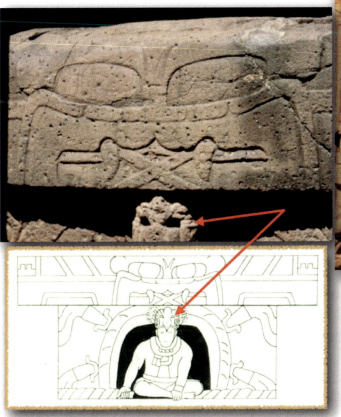

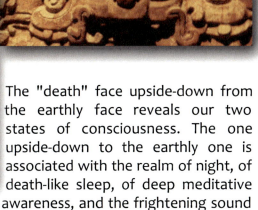

The "death" face upside-down from the earthly face reveals our two states of consciousness. The one upside-down to the earthly one is associated with the realm of night, of death-like sleep, of deep meditative awareness, and the frightening sound of the jaguar in the dark depths of the rainforest. Here the rainforest represents the dark, deep, inner, unseen realms of life and magic. These two realities need to become one in our soul growth for us to become our true celestial soul, who is only temporarily sojourning *purposefully* in this physical life. The way we live this life either enhances our soul-self and consciousness or confuses it. It also determines how conscious we will be during meditation, sleep, and eventually when the physical body-temple releases our soul through death. The next life is nourished by how well we live this life.

Reincarnation

The Maya believed in a *soul* life, a life that was eternal because the soul never dies. When the soul entered a physical body, it was bound to the body until the body no longer functioned (died) – in which case death of the body *released* the living soul. The living soul may then travel down through the Underworld (Xibalba) or up into any of the 13 Heavens (Aztecs and Toltecs also believed in 13 heavens, Kabbalah has 7). The soul was now a discarnate relative of its incarnate relatives, providing guidance and answering questions from the spirit world. Multiple incarnations were seen as a way of building a stronger, wiser soul who overcomes all darkness, illusion, and weakness. This concept is exemplified in the story of the Maize god in the *Popol Vuh* as it lives through cycles of birth, life, death, and rebirth. The Maize god and its various sets of twins face the challenges of the Dark Lords of the Underworld – who use confusion, deception, illusion, seemingly impossible-to-win trials and tests, and even trickery in achieving their many victories over the twins – that is, until the latest set of twins have become so much wiser, stronger, and magical than their previous incarnations that they defeat the Dark Lords. (see p. 33)

Souls were and remain the Children of God, however they lost their way as they experienced life with free will and relationships with other free-willed souls, as well as the temptations and illusions of the Dark Forces. Thus, early incarnations were strongly divine while later incarnations were more human and earthly. For example, Lord Pakal, great ruler of Palenqué, considered himself to be the reincarnation of a god, as a "godling" within the great Triad of God (the Mayan Trinity). The Triad was: God 1 (G1) from Heaven 6, an aspect of god from the unseen depths, as a deep "sea" god, expressing the infinite in the finite; God 2 (G2) a lightening god, an aspect of god that expresses the light to the darkness; and God 3 (G3) a fire god, an aspect of god who expresses the fire of the Spirit and the power of the jaguar!

In the illustration on the next page we see the lid to Lord Pakal sarcophagus, depicting his rising from physical death to his divinity among the heavens with the help of the Bird of Paradise, the Quetzal Bird on top of the World Tree, revealing the many influences and levels of consciousness! Life is eternal for our soul. It is temporary for our projected persona. Our soul lives on and on until it is one with the source of its life and consciousness.

This is the lid to Lord Pakal's sarcophagus, illustrated by Gary Keesler. Below is an illustration of a Mesoamerican scribe recording their fascinating stories for all of us to read and understand today, and hopefully find value for our lives.

Another Visual Training Book that You May Enjoy is:

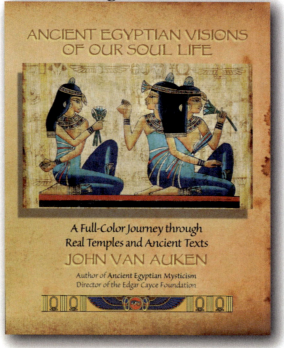

Living in the Light Publishing
P.O. Box 4942
Virginia Beach VA 23454-0942 USA

JohnVanAuken.com
JohnVanAukenNewsletter@gmail.com
Available through Amazon.com

Made in the USA
Middletown, DE
24 September 2024